CALIFORNIA TRAVELERS' TRIVIA

—historic and contemporary—

FABULOUS FIRSTS
FASCINATING FACTS
LEGENDARY LORE
ONE-OF-A-KIND ODDITIES
TANTALIZING TRIVIA

Bob Carter

TWODOT®
Guilford, Connecticut

An imprint of The Globe Pequot Press

"Curiosity is one of the permanent and certain characteristics of a vigorous intellect."

—Samuel Johnson British critic, poet, lexicographer (1709–1784)

Library of Congress Cataloging-in-Publication Data
Carter, Bob, 1932-
California travelers' trivia : historic and contemporary : fabulous firsts, fascinating facts, legendary lore, one-of-a-kind oddities, tantalizing trivia / Bob Carter.
p. cm.
ISBN 1-56044-954-3
1. California--Miscellanea. 2. California--History, Local--Miscellanea. I. Title.

F861.6 .C37 2001
979.4--dc21

00-045606

Manufactured in the United States of America
First Edition/First Printing

The information contained in this publication has been collected for entertainment purposes from a variety of sources believed reliable. However, since details are subject to change, there is no guarantee as to the accuracy of contents on any given date. While every effort has been made to confirm information, please note the author is not responsible for errors, lies, or exaggerations found in this labor of love.

About the Author

Bob Carter is a prolific, award-winning print and electronic media travel writer and columnist. He has served on the faculty of Pasadena City College; California State University, Los Angeles; and the University of Oregon. Carter has traveled tens of thousands of miles around the world collecting information for travel and food articles published in popular books, newspapers, magazines, and the world wide web. When not traveling, he resides in the desert region of southern California.

Books by Falcon Publishing

Food Festivals of Northern California: Traveler's Guide & Cookbook

Food Festivals of Southern California: Traveler's Guide & Cookbook

Food Festivals of Texas: Traveler's Guide & Cookbook

Books by Other Publishers

The Best of Central California: Main Roads & Side Trips

Soup's On! Hot Recipes from Cool Chefs (with Gail Hobbs)

Camper's Cookbook: Recipes with Campers in Mind

Introduction

California is an incredible state. From Antioch to Zuma Beach, the Golden State dazzles with one million and one unique and off-beat experiences. From the mountains to the sea and the desert to the cities, no other state offers the diverse ingredients one discovers in California.

During a long career as an educator and professional writer, it has been my personal hobby to collect a variety of fascinating facts, fabulous firsts, legendary lore, tantalizing trivia, and one-of-a-kind oddities about California. I collected them from all manner of people, places, and things and shared them with thousands of my friends, students, and readers. It has long been a dream to compile them to share with others. This book provides me that opportunity.

Any endeavor such as this requires support and assistance from dozens of people. It could not have been done without the enthusiastic help and contributions of numerous staff and volunteers at chambers of commerce, visitor information centers, attractions, and the State of California's Division of Tourism. In addition, California visitors and residents have shared their favorite facts with me and made significant contributions to the collection. I thank them all.

My editor, Charlene Patterson, has shepherded the content and idiosyncrasies of publishing; my highly supportive friend, Terry Poland, has contributed greatly with the compilation and the computer. Others too numerous to mention have given me the inspiration and wherewithal to undertake this labor of love.

I have added several related resources (see pages 138–40) for anyone interested in reading more about the trivia of the Golden State.

A

Agoura

Historians believe the Paramount Ranch, formerly owned by Paramount Pictures, is the best preserved complex of structures associated with the "Golden Age of Hollywood."

Alpine County

The eighth smallest of California's 58 counties, Alpine County has no high schools, ATMs, dentists, banks, or traffic lights.

Altadena

The International Banana Club Museum features the first and largest museum in the world devoted exclusively to the banana. It contains nearly 17,000 banana-related pieces in the collection.

Christmas Tree Lane features the oldest annual Christmas lighting display in southern California.

Amador City

Billed as the smallest incorporated city in the state in both population and area, the town's creek—and subsequently the town—was named after gold miner Jose Maria Amador. The town has a population of about 200 and contains a total of 187 acres—30 zoned for residential use, 9 for commercial use, and 3 for institutional use.

Anaheim

Long before Disneyland became a major destination, Anaheim was the wine capital of California. It remained so until the late nineteenth century when a blight attacked the vines and local farmers began the orange industry in the area that became Orange County.

Disneyland's hometown is Anaheim.

Disneyland opened on July 17, 1955, with 18 major attractions. Today there are more than 60 attractions.

More than 20,000 gallons of paint are used each year to give the park a better-than-new look.

There are 19 million gallons of water in the park's ten bodies of water.

There are more than 100,000 light bulbs used in Disneyland including 11,000 "rim lights" used to outline the buildings on Main Street, U.S.A.

All the twinkling lights in the facades on Main Street are replaced on a schedule based on the average life of the bulb.

The streets of the park are washed and steam-cleaned each day after the park closes.

ROBERT HOLMES/CAL TOUR

Sleeping Beauty's Castle in Disneyland.

There are more than 800 species of plants from more than 40 nations in the park.

More than 25 different varieties of grasses are found throughout the facility.

Each year approximately 1 million annuals are planted.

The Mickey Mouse flower "portrait" located at the Main Entrance is replanted nine times a year.

Recycled in one year are 2.4 million pounds of cardboard; 512,000 pounds of office paper; and 6,550 pounds of aluminum cans.

In one year Disneyland guests buy 4 million hamburgers, 1.6 million hot dogs, 3.4 million orders of fries, 1.5 million servings of popcorn, 3.2 million servings of ice cream, 1.2 million gallons of soft drinks, and 2.8 million churros.

More than 4,000 different costumes have been designed and produced for entertainment in the facility.

During the year the park receives over 7 million phone calls. The most frequently called person is Mickey Mouse.

Disneyland uses 26 million hand towels in its restrooms each year. Additionally, park attendants use 1,000 brooms, 500 dust pans, and 3,000 mops each year to keep the park clean. Approximately 30 tons of trash are collected during a busy day.

Angels Camp

Popularly known as the "Frog Jumping Capital of the World," this gold country community provided the setting for the Samuel Clemens short story "The Celebrated Jumping Frog of Calaveras County." On one of his regular visits to the bar at the Angels Hotel, Clemens overheard the tale and, using the nom de plume Mark Twain, penned the story that made him a household name. It tells of a barroom wager concerning whose frog can jump the farthest and the trick played by the owner of the winning frog. Twain's partially replicated rustic cabin is located a short distance from town. Today the historic city hosts the annual the Jumping Frog Jubilee.

Aptos

Originally the one-hundred-foot-long Aptos Creek Covered Bridge was not covered. The bridge was covered later to add charm to the village.

Arcadia

There is a city law on the books giving peacocks the right of way to cross any street, including driveways.

Arcata

Built in 1914, the Minor Theatre reigns as one of the oldest continuously operating motion picture theaters in the nation.

Fun facts

- The inspiration for the state name was Califia, a mythical paradise located in a Spanish romance story written by Montalvo in 1510.
- Between 1840 and 1860 more than 200,000 people traveled the overland trails to California. This is considered the largest peacetime migration in history.
- In 1849, one year prior to statehood, California was 2,200 miles away from the United States.

Arnold

With a width of 24 feet, Calaveras Big Trees State Park's Louis Agassiz Tree flourishes as the tree with the widest diameter in the California state parks system.

Arroyo Grande

Chase Olive Company claims to be the largest and oldest gourmet olive company on the West Coast. It was founded in 1960 and offers olive tastings.

The only one of its kind in California, the Swinging Bridge was originally constructed in 1875. Newton Short's land was divided by Arroyo Grande Creek and the bridge linked the two sides. The bridge is 171 feet long and hangs 40 feet above the creek.

Atwater

Castle Air Museum has the largest display of military aircraft in the state.

Avalon (See Santa Catalina Island)

B

Baker

Built in 1991, the world's tallest thermometer towers 134 feet above town. It commemorates the highest temperature ever recorded in North America: 134 degrees.

The Country Store in Baker has sold more winning California State Lottery tickets than any other outlet in the state.

Bakersfield

California's oldest motorsports track is the Bakersfield Speedway. The facility's annual Turkey Night USAC Midget Grand Prix provides the second-longest-running open wheel event in the nation. The oldest open wheel event is the Indy 500.

More honey comes from southern California than from the rest of the United States. Most of the bee ranches in southern California are located around Bakersfield.

Country singer Merle Haggard was born in Bakersfield. His most famous song is *Okie from Muskogee.* Another Bakersfielder is Frank Gifford, a well-known football player and sports broadcaster. Musician Buck Owens was born in Sherman, Texas, and moved to Bakersfield with his family in the early 1950s. He and his family reside on a large ranch outside the city.

Balboa

Balboa's first historical landmark, the Balboa Pavilion, built in 1905, still stands on the bay.

A 50-year-old restored merry-go-round, Ferris wheel, bumper cars, and a scary dark ride can be found at the Fun Zone Amusement Park.

Fun facts

State Animal: Grizzly Bear

The Grizzly Bear appears on the state flag and the Great State Seal, but it is now extinct in California.

Ballard

Established in 1880, Ballard is the oldest town in the Santa Ynez Valley. Built in 1883, Ballard School remains the oldest school still in use in the state. It is used by local children in kindergarten through eighth grade. Popularly known as the Little Red Schoolhouse, the building hasn't always been red; it was formerly painted railroad yellow.

Barstow

The Black Mountain area has more than 10,000 Native American rock art petroglyphs.

To satisfy hungry travelers, the world's first Del Taco was started in Barstow in 1961 by brothers Tony and Ed Hackbarth.

Many cities along famous Route 66 gave the name Main Street to their major thoroughfare. Barstow is the last town to maintain a vestige of Route 66 still named Main Street.

When railroading was in its glamour days, Fred Harvey, noted hotel and restaurant entrepreneur, set up and operated a series of dining and boarding locations along the Santa Fe train line. In Barstow, he opened Casa Del Desierto. Still in existence, the building is considered the best surviving reminder of California's Harvey days.

Benicia

The only surviving state capitol building dating back before Sacramento was given the honor is in Benicia. The restored structure is located on the grounds of Capitol State Park. Pre-Sacramento capitol buildings formerly located in San Jose and Vallejo no longer exist.

Beverly Hills

Technically, one cannot be traditionally born or buried in Beverly Hills. The city has no hospital or cemetery. There are also no billboards or visible telephone or power wires.

All Beverly Hills zip codes are on the list of the top fifteen wealthiest cities in the United States.

Beverly Hills has been recognized as "Tree City USA" and has more trees than inhabitants. Approximately one tree per resident grows in the public zones of the city and nearly triple that grow within private properties.

From 1912 to 1916 Beverly Hills had its own baseball team, called the "Bean Eaters" for the lima bean fields in the area.

In the early nineteenth century, 20,000 pounds of honey were shipped annually from beekeepers located in Benedict Canyon, north of Sunset Boulevard.

There are more Rolls Royces owned by Beverly Hills residents than the rest of America combined.

In 1920, Will Rogers became the first honorary mayor of the city.

Valet parking, an idea that originated in Beverly Hills, first began on the city's famous Rodeo Drive.

Fun facts

- The California Gold Rush yielded 125 million ounces of gold—that's worth more than $50 billion by today's standards.
- California's population grew from 14,000 to 223,000 between 1848 and 1852.

The well-known William Morris Agency is lauded as the oldest and most established theatrical agency in the world.

The oldest tree in the city is a Morton Bay fig from Australia. It is more than 80 years old and 65 feet tall.

Big Bear

The Dynastar Performance Center at Big Bear Mountain Resort is the only ski-in, ski-out test center of its kind. For a small fee, the center allows skiers to test all the skis they want during a four-hour period. The back door opens and skiers glide in, stop over a pit, step into a new pair of skis, and ski out.

The lake at Big Bear is the largest mountain lake in southern California. The reservoir is 7 miles long and 1 mile across at its widest point and has a maximum depth of 72 feet and more than 23 miles of shoreline.

After 20 years of planning, the Big Bear Discovery Center opened in 1998. Located on the north shore of Big Bear Lake, the center is considered a model for forest visitor centers across the nation. Its highlights include visitor information, wildlife exhibits, self- and ranger-guided walks and tours, and outdoor recreational activities.

The bald eagle population in southern California was exterminated in the late 1950s. Reintroduction began in the 1980s on Catalina Island. Now the Bear Valley basin supports the largest wintering bald eagle population in southern California. Normally eagles arrive in late November and stay in the region until early April. Over the past 20 years the area's population of the national symbol has fluctuated from lows of 10 to 12 to highs of 35 to 40.

Big Pine

Reaching 14,494 feet at its summit, Mount Whitney, located in Inyo National Forest, prevails as the highest point in the contiguous United States.

Ancient Bristlecone Pine Forest is located 23 miles east of town on the slopes of White Mountain. Having survived more than 40 centuries, the ancient gnarled and twisted trees exceed the age of the oldest giant sequoia by 1,500 years. Methuselah, the oldest known tree in the world, is a bristlecone pine believed to be 4,700 years old. It stands at Schulman Grove, part of the Ancient Bristlecone Pine Forest. Each bristlecone pine, from young seedling to ancient relic, has an individual character. The rings of these ancient trees have been used to recalibrate Carbon 14 dating.

Big Sur

It is not uncommon for prisoners to be granted time off their sentences in exchange for contributing public work. Big Sur's Bixby Bridge was built by prisoners eager to obtain time off. At 714 feet long and 260 feet high, the single-span bridge is one of the world's highest of its type.

McWay Creek Falls, which drops 80 feet and is the tallest waterfall in the California state parks system, performs at Julia Pfeiffer Burns Park.

Bishop

Popularly known as the "Mule Capital of the World," the city holds an annual Mule Days celebration. With an average of 200 entries, the mule parade is considered the longest nonmotorized parade in the world.

In 1883 the Carson and Colorado Railroad provided the only dependable means of transportation in and out of the Owens Valley. The train that traveled through the valley was dubbed "The Slim Princess." The original narrow-gauge train stands as a feature of the Laws Railroad Museum and Historical Site.

Blythe

Centuries ago Native Americans living in the lower Colorado River Valley created gigantic human, animal, and geometric figures known as intaglios. The best site to see them is about 15 miles north of Blythe, where there are six distinct figures in three locations. They include a human figure at each location and an animal figure at two locations.

A city law on the books prohibits the wearing of cowboy boots by those who don't own at least two cows.

Bodfish

Silver City Ghost Town contains nearly 25 historic buildings dating back to the mid-1800s. Renovation and restoration has been underway since 1990. The town serves as a popular movie and television filming site.

ANNE MARIE NOVINGER

Bristlecone Pine.

Bodie

The largest unrestored ghost town in the American West, Bodie State Historic Park, remains in a condition of arrested decay. Located along a bumpy dirt road, the isolated town contains remnants from the Eastern Sierra's greatest mining boom.

Boron

The U.S. Borax open pit mine operates as the largest in California. It is 0.75 mile wide, 1.5 miles long, and over 650 feet deep. If filled with water, the pit would hold 66 billion gallons.

Borrego Springs

The resort community exists within the nation's largest state park. Anza-Borrego Desert State Park contains 640,000 acres of nature trails and scenic and recreational wonders.

Anza-Borrego Desert State Park is one of the hottest locations in the desert. Summer temperatures reach the range of 120 degrees.

Anne Marie Novinger

Bodie State Historic Park remains in a condition of arrested decay.

Boulder Creek

Located nine miles northwest of Boulder Creek, Big Basin Redwoods State Park is the oldest state park in California.

Brentwood

The 125,000-square-foot Skirball Cultural Center and Museum contains exhibits celebrating and examining the Jewish American experience. It holds the world's second largest collection of wimples.

The richest museum in the world is the Getty Center. The Getty is the world's most comprehensive arts and education facility.

Bridgeport

A controversy continues concerning whether or not the Bridgeport Bridge is the longest single-span covered bridge in existence. Portal to portal it measures 233 feet, but the clear span—the distance between piers—is 298 feet. An official measuring in 1938 concluded the Bridgeport Bridge was 2 feet shorter than the Old Blondheim Bridge in New York. All agree that the bridge has the longest roof line.

Buellton

It was 1924 when Anton and Juliette Andersen opened the Electrical Café. Their split pea soup brought in travelers from Highway 101. Newspaper writers (including Hedda Hopper), celebrities, and dignitaries stopped at the restaurant on their way to visit William Randolph Hearst in San Simeon. They made the little café a popular roadside stop. Although the old-time charm is long gone, the restaurant continues to serve the internationally known split pea soup. Known now as Andersen's, the restaurant is probably the world's foremost pea purchaser. In the early 1930s a cartoonist introduced Hap-Pea and Pea-Wee, and the characters still serve as the restaurant's two chef icons.

Buena Park

Buena Park offers five major family-oriented tourist attractions within walking distance of each other. That's more than any other city in California.

Knott's Berry Farm's hometown is Buena Park.

The theme park began as a small produce stand situated along a country road. Camp Snoopy is the world's first area in any amusement park designed exclusively for children.

The world's largest single-location chicken restaurant, Mrs. Knott's Chicken Dinner Restaurant, seats 1,000 patrons at a time and serves more than 1.5 million people annually.

Supreme Scream is the world's tallest descending thrill-ride and the tallest structure in Orange County. The 312-foot-tall ride opened in July 1998.

At 4,533 feet in length, GhostRider is the longest wooden roller coaster in the western United States.

Bigfoot Rapids is the longest manmade whitewater river in California.

Fun facts

State Bird: California Quail

The California Quail, noted for its strength and adaptability, is found throughout the state.

Opened in 1955, Ghost Town & Calico Railroad still operates daily and has the world's worst crime rate. The train is held up by Knott's bandits 10,000 times annually.

The park is the birthplace of the boysenberry, funnel cake, and churro.

The park is the world's only amusement/theme park with a church offering Sunday worship services. Church of the Reflections congregation members are not charged park admission to attend church.

Perilous Plunge is the tallest and steepest water ride in the world.

Burbank

Some of the scenes in which the dinosaur terrorizes San Diego in the movie *Jurassic Park: The Lost World* were actually filmed in downtown Burbank.

First National Pictures began its motion picture studio in Burbank in the 1920s. Later the studio was acquired by Warner Brothers. In 1939 the Walt Disney Company brought its animation film kingdom to the community, and NBC made its presence known on the Burbank scene in 1951.

Burbank Airport served as Los Angeles's primary airport until the 1950s.

In the early 1950s, Debbie Reynolds, actress and entertainer, was crowned Miss Burbank.

Burlingame

There is a city law on the books making it illegal to spit except on baseball diamonds.

Buttonwillow

South of town, native tule elk may be viewed at Tule Elk State Reserve. The reserve is home to a rare species of elk unique to California.

Butte County

California's first suspension bridge, the Bidwell Canyon Bridge, was built in 1856. It was relocated to avoid submergence when Lake Oroville was developed, and it is still in use.

Bidwell Park covers 3,600 acres, making it the largest municipal park west of the Mississippi.

At more than 54 pounds, a gold nugget found in the county is the largest ever discovered in the state. When refined it yielded 49.5 pounds of pure gold.

C

Cabazon

Two nearly lifesize dinosaur replicas stand out tall and large in the tiny desert community. Sculpted by Claude Bell, the brontosaurus and tyrannosaurus rex can be seen from the nearby freeway. There's a museum and gift shop in the tummy of one of the creatures.

Fun facts

· A California law makes it a misdemeanor to shoot any kind of game from a moving vehicle unless the target is a whale.

Calabasas

In 1983 the Plummer House, known as the oldest house in Hollywood, was moved to the grounds of the Leonis Adobe in Calabasas. The home was originally part of Plummer Park, an enormous ranch owned by Major Henry Hancock. The ranch was famous for its tar pits and skeletons of prehistoric animals.

California City

Located in the Mojave Desert, the 25,000-acre California Desert Tortoise Natural Area protects a significant number of threatened desert tortoises, the state's reptile.

Calipatria

The city has an 182-foot-long flagpole. This is the exact number of feet the town is below sea level.

Calistoga

It took a pioneering spirit to settle the West, and Calistoga's earliest citizens were among the most hearty and eccentric. Among them was California's first millionaire, Sam Brannon, who set out to develop the area as a first-class resort and named the town in the process. Author Robert Louis Stevenson recuperated in Calistoga's healthy climate while gathering information for two books.

Silverado Museum contains nearly 7,000 artifacts important to the life of author and poet Robert Louis Stevenson. In the 1880s Stevenson and his wife spent their honeymoon in Napa Valley.

Calistoga Depot is considered to be the oldest surviving railroad depot in the state.

Old Faithful Geyser of California performs at regular intervals and the area is as geothermally active today as when it was first discovered.

Cambria

Built in 1928, Nit Wit Ridge is a folk art house located in a residential neighborhood in Cambria. The unique construction of the building incorporates native materials, rocks and mortar, seashells, eclectic findings, and timbers. The house is the creation of Arthur Harold Beal, a Cambria pioneer.

The Friends of the Piedras Blancas Lighthouse Lens preserved the lens for public viewing. The original Fresnel lens, reportedly one of two "first order" lenses in the world, is exhibited in the lantern room at Pinedorado Grounds.

Canby

Remnants of the Lassen Trail are still visible west of town. The trail was used extensively during the California gold rush when more than 21,000 people came to the state. A vast number of them used this trail.

Carlsbad

Carlsbad is home to the most extensive ranunculus fields in the world. Visitors are encouraged to stroll and view the colorful flowers up close. The bird of paradise was first developed commercially in Carlsbad and is the city's official flower.

The first LEGOLAND park in North America opened in 1999. It features 40 rides and attractions including a collection of 1,000 buildings and famous landmarks built with 20 million LEGO bricks.

Held annually on the same date, the Spring Village Faire and the Fall Village Fair are the largest, concurrent, single-day street festivals in California. Both feature hundreds of exhibitors, international food booths, and entertainment

Carmel

Former residents of this seaside hamlet include poet Robinson Jeffers and the well-known environmentalist and photographer Ansel Adams. Actor Clint Eastwood was formerly elected and served as mayor.

The village exudes uniqueness in several ways. It is only 1 square mile in size, has no street lights or sidewalks, and the beach is unadulterated by commercial development. There is no mail delivery; homes are known by name and have no addresses.

Legend has it Robert Louis Stevenson received his inspiration for *Treasure Island* while walking on the beach near Point Lobos.

Carson Hill

The largest gold nugget ever found in the western hemisphere was unearthed in 1854 at the gold mine located in Carson Hill.

Castroville

The "Artichoke Capital of the World" contains thousands of acres devoted to the plant's cultivation. In 1947 a young woman by the

Fun facts

State Colors: Yale Blue and Golden Yellow

Blue and gold ribbons formerly adorned the Great State Seal. Blue and gold are also the spirit colors of the prestigious University of California education system.

name of Norma Jean was crowned Castroville's first "Artichoke Queen." She later gained fame as actress Marilyn Monroe. Castroville produces 85 percent of the nation's artichokes.

Chester

Lake Almanor is the largest lake in Plumas County. It is located in Lassen National Forest and covers nearly 30,000 acres.

Chico

Bidwell Mansion, located at Bidwell Mansion State Historic Park, has the honor of being the first mansion in the state with an indoor bathroom.

Open daily, the National YoYo Museum includes extensive examples of early yo-yos including the world's largest wooden yo-yo, which weighs 256 pounds and stands 50 inches tall. Each year the museum hosts a national competition considered America's premier yo-yo contest. The contest features the country's best players exhibiting their most difficult yo-yo tricks.

ROBERT HOLMES/CALTOUR

Honey Run Covered Bridge.

The community provided some of the sites for several noted films, including *Gone with the Wind, The Great Waltz,* and *The Adventures of Robin Hood.*

Located just outside the city, the Honey Run Covered Bridge, built in 1894, is the only three-level covered bridge in the nation with three distinctive roof lines. An annual pancake breakfast fundraiser is held the first Sunday in June.

There is a city law on the books imposing a $500 fine for detonating a nuclear device within the city limits.

Chino

The Planes of Fame air museum was the first aviation museum west of the Mississippi.

Cima

Cima Dome is called the most symmetrical natural dome in the Unites States. The small town of Cima and the dome are located in the Mojave National Preserve, which is also home to the world's largest Joshua tree forest. The preserve begins about 60 miles west of Barstow and borders the Nevada state line.

Claremont

Rancho Santa Ana Botanic Garden is the largest California garden specializing in native plants. The 86-acre garden is planted with more than 6,000 wild species and is the only garden in the state devoted exclusively to the conservation, preservation, and display of California's native flora.

Clearlake

First, to avoid confusion, Clearlake, the town, is spelled as one word; the lake's name is spelled as two. The city is known as the

"Bass Capital of the West." Clear Lake is recognized as the largest natural freshwater lake located completely within California's borders and as the oldest lake in North America.

The area of geysers near the lake is the world's largest geothermal region.

Cleone

MacKerricher State Park and Oceano Dunes State Vehicular Recreation Area both spotlight the state's most extensive sand dunes located in the California state parks system.

Coalinga

The Harris Ranch is famous for its horned toads and black gold. It is also known as the "Iron Zoo" for the oil rigs located on the property with animals painted on them. The celebration of Horned Toad Derby Days features a toad race, barbecue, and special ceremonies.

Colma

The city wears the banner "City of the Dead." The story goes that when San Francisco developers discovered the high value of the

Fun facts

- Coast redwoods *(sequoia sempervirens)* are found only in California along a narrow coastal strip between Monterey and the northern California border.
- With a wingspan of about 9 feet and an average weight of 20 pounds, the baldheaded California condor is the largest flying bird in North America.

area's residential land, they argued for moving the city's cemeteries to Colma, a rural location with less expensive land. In 1900 San Francisco passed an ordinance prohibiting burials except in Mission Dolores and the presidio cemeteries. Dignitaries finding their resting place in Colma include William Randolph Hearst, George Moscone, Levi Strauss, Wyatt Earp, and Tina Turner's pet dog.

Columbia

On March 27, 1850, gold was discovered in what is now the well-preserved gold rush village of Columbia. The town keeps its past alive by offering stagecoach rides, gold panning, and performances by costumed artisans demonstrating skills associated with the California gold rush.

Colusa

The Colusa County Courthouse, erected in 1861, is the oldest courthouse in the Sacramento Valley.

Corning

The "Olive Capital of the United States" is the site of the world's largest plant for canning black table olives.

Coronado

Hotel del Coronado is known for its opulent Victorian decor and architecture. The three oldest operating Otis elevators in the world are at the hotel and have been running since the hotel opened in 1888. In 1904 the hotel introduced the world's first electrically lighted outdoor Christmas tree, a Norfolk Island (Star) Pine adorned with 250 lights. The first water polo game in the United States was staged at the hotel in 1907.

Coronado's flat, wide, expansive beach serves as the running ground for United States Navy SEALs most mornings at 7 A.M. The beach is anchored to the north by Naval Air Stations North Island, the birthplace of United States naval aviation, and to the south by the Hotel del Coronado, a national historic landmark.

Costa Mesa

Costa Mesa is the home of the largest privately funded performing arts center in the United States.

Coulterville

America's largest canyon oak, the Jordan Oak, has a trunk diameter of 32.5 feet. The large trunk then splits into 6 trunks. The oak is estimated to be between 300 and 500 years old.

ROBERT HOLMES/CALTOUR

Hotel del Coronado.

The Hotel Jeffery is the oldest hotel in the state; it has been owned by one family since 1851. Former guests include John Muir and President Theodore Roosevelt.

Crescent City

The largest wave (tsunami) to ever wash ashore in California destroyed 56 blocks of Crescent City on March 28, 1964. The wave reached as high as 20.7 feet.

The small seaside community is known as the "Shrimp Capital of California."

Battery Point Lighthouse, one of the first lighthouses on the West Coast, was completed in 1855.

Jedediah Smith Redwoods State Park, named for the famous mountaineer, is the northernmost of California's 30 redwood parks. In 1826 Smith became the first American to travel overland from the Mississippi River to California. He was the first white person to cross the Sierra Nevada. The state park contains the last major river without a dam in the state.

One of the most important nautical finds in California history is the double sidewheeled steamship that lies submerged off the coast of Crescent City.

Point Saint George Lighthouse is the tallest and most expensive lighthouse ever built in the United States. After ten years of construction that cost more than $700,000, the 146-foot-tall lighthouse opened in 1891.

The hull of the tanker S.S. *Emidio* lies off the coast of Crescent City and represents the first casualty of the imperial Japanese submarine action on the state's coastal waters.

Cucamonga Valley

The valley once boasted the largest concentration of vineyards in the nation. The land is now covered by suburbs, but three local wineries remain.

D

Daly City

Daly City is recognized as the location of the battle that ended dueling in California. The last duel took place between United States Senator David C. Broderick and Chief Justice David S. Terry.

Dana Point

Author Richard Dana (1851–1882) was the inspiration for the name of this beach city he used as a retreat. His popular book *Two Years before the Mast* appears on the reading list of numerous California schools.

Danville

Mount Diablo State Park can be entered through Danville or Walnut Creek.

Fun facts

State Dance: The West Coast Swing

The West Coast Swing came into being in the early 1930s in response to the new era of music then sweeping the nation.

Mount Diablo State Park's summit is 3,849 feet above sea level and offers a sweeping panorama. More of the earth's surface can be seen from the mountain than from any other peak in the world except Mount Kilimanjaro in Africa.

Davenport

In 1914 the Davenport jailhouse was built to protect the locals from marauding criminals. Ironically, the town was already so safe and crime-free that the new jail was built with only two tiny cells. For more than 20 years the only people held in the cells were one drunk sent there to dry out overnight and two young boys caught stealing horses. The residents eagerly point out that these culprits were from a different town.

Death Valley

Shoshones first settled this desert land.

Death Valley got its apt name in 1849 when Juliette Brier and several companions traveled through the area in search of California's gold. They encountered unbearable temperatures and terrain and four members of their party died. The travelers began to refer to the region as Death Valley and the name stuck.

Furnace Creek Golf Course boasts having the lowest golf course in the world. The course is 210 feet below sea level.

The 680-foot-high Eureka Dunes are the tallest sand dunes in the state.

At 11,049 feet, Telescope Peak in the Panamint Range towers as the valley's highest point.

Dante's View is without peer anywhere in the world. From this point, 5,475 feet above sea level, it is possible to view the lowest point in Death Valley and, in the distance, the snowcapped peaks of the High Sierra.

Death Valley National Park is the largest national park in the contiguous United States. It contains more than 3.3 million acres of land and houses Scotty's Castle, the grandiose residence of one of California's most unique personalities. Walter Scott, born in 1872 and also called "Death Valley Scotty," remains Death Valley's greatest legend for his flamboyant and outrageous character. After traveling the world with the Buffalo Bill Wild West Show for more than a decade, Scotty began gold prospecting. He convinced several wealthy businesspeople he had claim to a gold mine worth a fortune in Death Valley. Unfortunately his prospecting in Death Valley provided little gold. He was instrumental in convincing others to construct Death Valley Ranch in the late 1920s. Scotty lived at the ranch for the last two years of his life. He was laid to rest on a hill overlooking the famous home that bears his name.

Badwater is the lowest point in the Western Hemisphere. Its elevation descends 282 feet below sea level.

Robert Holmes/CalTour

Death Valley National Park.

Death Valley's highest temperature of 134 degrees, lowest temperature of 15 degrees, and record amount of rain—4.54 inches—were all recorded in the year 1913. All of these remain as records today.

In 1974, Death Valley had a high temperature of over 100 degrees for 134 consecutive days. The summer of 1994 saw 31 days over 120 degrees and 97 days over 110 degrees.

Dorrington

The city is home to the second largest sugar pine in the world. The tree boasts a circumference of 32 feet and is 222 feet tall.

Dorris

The tallest flagpole in the United States towers over the town. Measuring 36 inches wide at its base and 5.6 inches at the top, the pole is buried in 22 feet of concrete and can withstand wind reaching 100 miles per hour. The pole's flying flag measures 30 feet by 60 feet. It is 200 feet tall.

Drytown

This historic town, founded in 1848, was the first place in Amador County where gold was discovered. Dry Creek, the site of Drytown, was probably the first creek panned in the county. Once home to 26 saloons, the town did not get its name because it was "dry" of booze.

E

Eagle Rock

The natural phenomenon that gave the town of Eagle Rock its name can be viewed from the nearby freeway. When the sun is in the right position, the huge landmark hill features an outcropping resembling a soaring eagle.

Earlimart

Earlimart is California's only town originally funded, financed, and governed by African Americans. The town was founded in 1908. Today the town is known as Colonel Allensworth State Historic Park.

Encinitas

Quail Botanical Gardens has the largest variety of bamboo on display in North America. The gardens also have the largest collection of hibiscus on the West Coast.

Fun facts

- The Frisbee was invented in California. In 1955 Richard Knerr and Arthur Melin, co-owners of Whamo-O, a small mail-order company, saw a disk flying through the air on a California beach. The owner of the disk told them he had purchased it at the Los Angeles County Fair. The two Wham-O owners contacted the man selling the disk, negotiated the rights to it, and began manufacturing it. The Pluto Platter was introduced in January 1957. Later it was renamed the Frisbee.

Escondido

Escondido Historical Society owns and operates the only blacksmith shop in California offering classes and instruction.

Eureka

There are more Victorian buildings per capita in Eureka than in any other incorporated city in California. The town has more than 10,000 Victorian buildings, each with more ornate detail than the next.

Built in 1936 over the Elk River, Berta's Ranch covered bridge is the most westerly covered bridge in the United States. Almost an exact twin, the Zane's Ranch covered bridge, built a quarter mile upriver, is the second most westerly covered bridge in the country. Both bridges are 52 feet long and built of native redwood, which was inexpensive and plentiful at the time the bridges were constructed.

ROBERT HOLMES/CALTOUR

Carson Mansion.

Fort Humboldt was built to protect early California settlers. In 1853 the fort served as the headquarters of a young Ulysses S. Grant, who was known as Sam Grant while he served as a captain at the fort.

Proclaimed the most photographed Victorian building in the world, the Carson Mansion was built between 1884 and 1886.

The first brewery in the United States founded and operated by women is Eureka's Lost Coast Brewery.

Sixty percent of the tallest trees in the world may be viewed along the 31-mile-long Avenue of the Giants Scenic Drive through Humboldt Redwoods State Park.

F

Fallbrook

Deer Park Auto Museum boasts the world's largest display of American production convertibles.

Known as the "Avocado Capital of the World," Fallbrook hosts the annual Avocado Festival in April. More avocados are grown in the region than any other county in the nation.

The world's largest burrito was made at La Caesta restaurant and is recorded in the *Guinness Book of World Records*.

Felton

Built in 1892 from local timber, Felton Covered Bridge is 34 feet tall at its peak, making it the tallest covered bridge in the United States. One explanation for the extraordinary height is that it was built to accommodate a fully loaded lumber wagon.

Ferndale

The Ferndale Bridge leading into town is poised over the Eel River. The bridge was built in 1911, and it is the oldest reinforced concrete bridge in existence.

The oldest continuously running county fair in California is the Humboldt County Fair which is held each year in Ferndale. The fair has been running for more than 100 years.

Fiddletown

At one time the number of Chinese living in the town was surpassed only by the number living in San Francisco.

The town possibly got its name from a group of Missourians who brought their fiddles along when they trekked west in search of gold.

Robert Holmes/CalTour

Felton Covered Bridge.

The world's largest fiddle hangs in the Fiddletown Community Center. The wooden instrument measures 15 feet long.

Famous author Bret Harte wrote about the city in *An Episode of Fiddletown.*

Folsom

The town is the site of one of the oldest Wells Fargo assay offices and the Folsom Powerhouse, which produced the first commercial application of electricity.

Fort Bragg

The Weller House Inn serves as the only residence on the Mendocino coast listed on the National Registry of Historic Places. The inn also has a 51-foot-tall water tower—the tallest structure in town. The tower houses the highest hot tub in California.

Each year in September the city honors the state's lumberjacks. Paul Bunyan Days features fiddling contests, logging shows, carving, crafts, and the Paul Bunyan parade.

Noyo Harbor produces and touts the world's largest annual salmon barbecue; it's held on July 4.

The Skunk Train celebrates being the oldest passenger excursion train in California. It began operation in 1885 and contains the only self-propelled passenger train vehicles still in regular service in the United States. The train also delivers mail to Fort Bragg and surrounding communities.

Fort Tejon

During the Civil War, Fort Tejon was used by Union soldiers. Today the fort is a historic site. The site contains a grove of 500-year-old oak trees. From April to October, authentic military reenactments are held on the first Sunday of the month.

Fortuna

Since 1921 this town has held an annual rodeo, which makes it the location of the oldest rodeo in northwestern California. The week-long August event was started by a group of cattlemen who called themselves "roughriders."

Fossil Falls

Accessible via the 0.3-mile-long Big Falls Trail, Fossil Falls tumbles nearly 500 feet as southern California's tallest waterfall.

French Camp

In French Camp, not far from Bridgeport State Park, a plaque honors the world's first long-distance telephone line. It extended 58 miles to French Lake.

Fresno

The varied nature of the Fresno community is reflected in a list of prominent Fresnans. The late Pulitzer Prize–winning author William Saroyan was born in Fresno. (Each year a major festival is

Fun facts

State Fish: California Golden Trout

This trout species, *Salmo aqua-bonita,* is only found in the icy streams of the High Sierra and is native to no other state.

held to highlight his life and career.) New York Mets pitcher Tom Seaver and singer/actress Cher both called Fresno home. Indianapolis 500 winner Bill Vucovich; movie director Sam Peckinpah; Olympic decathlon winner Rafer Johnson; and Colonel Gregory "Pappy" Boyington hailed from the area. The world's only armless aviator is native Fresnan Loxia Thornton.

In the 1960s Fulton Street was closed to traffic and became the nation's first pedestrian mall.

Fashion Fair is considered the nation's first enclosed shopping mall.

The largest continuous vineyard in the United States is in Fresno. It contains 5,200 acres and produces 6,500 tons of grapes a year.

Fresno County

A small village known as Rootville, renamed Millerton, became the Fresno County seat in 1856.

More agricultural goods are produced in the county than in any other in the nation.

Fun facts

· The most popular tattoos in the men's California prison system are the words "Harley Davidson" and the Harley Davidson motorcycle logo.

· The first seedless watermelon was developed in California.

· The sound barrier was first broken in the sky over California by Brigadier General Chuck Yeager.

The county's first jail was built for a mere $6,000 but was so flimsy it couldn't hold prisoners. Another jail was built for $24,000 and was the only building to withstand the Christmas Eve flood that occurred soon after it was built. Incidentally, the first person to be incarcerated in the new jail was the contractor who built it. He was charged with murder during an election dispute.

Fresno County's only public execution occurred in 1893 when Dr. Frank O. Vincent was hanged for the murder of his wife. Formal invitations were sent out for the occasion. The event is thought to be the last public hanging in California.

Reputed to be the most corrupt politician in Fresno County history, vice-leader Joseph Spinney was mayor for only ten minutes.

Friant

Fort Miller, now inundated by Millerton Lake, was home to the first recorded religious services in the Fresno area. The 1855 service was conducted by Right Reverend William Ingraham Kip, the first Protestant Episcopal Bishop of California.

Fresno County's first courthouse was moved brick by brick to its present location on higher ground when the region was flooded to create Millerton Lake State Recreation Area.

Fullerton

Fullerton Municipal Airport is recognized as the oldest and largest general aviation field in Orange County.

G

Garden Grove

A 1.5-mile stretch of land provides an enclave of Vietnamese culture where approximately 150,000 Vietnamese live and work. The area has the largest concentration of Vietnamese outside of Asia.

Gilroy

The "Garlic Capital of the World" plays host to the annual Garlic Festival, unquestionably the nation's stinkiest food fair. The Christopher Ranch in Gilroy is the nation's largest garlic grower, processor, and shipper. The ranch distributes more than 25 million pounds of fresh garlic annually.

Glen Ellen

Author and adventurer Jack London was America's highest paid author in his day. He authored 51 books, including the famous *Call of the Wild*, and 193 short stories. The 800-acre Jack London State Historic Park is located on what was once London's Beauty Ranch.

Fun facts

State Flag: The Bear Flag

The great flag of California was first raised in 1846 by American settlers during an uprising against Mexican rule. Although the California Republic—which the flag represents—was short lived, the flag still symbolizes love of freedom and perseverance.

The site contains the cottage where he wrote, London's gravesite, outbuildings, and the impressive ruins of the burned-out Wolf House.

Glendale

The only known annual Blessing of the Cars event in the world is hosted by Glendale. During the special event a priest anoints and prays for the safety of cars and their owners and drivers.

The first paved runways located west of the Rocky Mountains were found at the Glendale Grand Central Air Terminal. It was at this airport that "Wrong Way" Douglas Corrigan built the airplane he used in his unauthorized international flight.

Grass Valley

One of the oldest and richest hardrock gold mines may be viewed at Empire Mine State Historic Park. At this site miners extracted nearly 6 million ounces of gold from 367 miles of tunnels dug into Ophir Hill. The park includes historic equipment, buildings, mine-shafts, and the William Bourne Junior home, built in 1897.

Gridley

The small community is recognized as the "Kiwi Capital of America."

Groveland

Iron Door Saloon, built in 1852, claims to be the oldest drinking establishment in California.

Hemet

The Ramona Pageant is the official California state outdoor play. Set on an early California rancho, the love story of Ramona and Alessandro portrays the tragic treatment of California's native people in the nineteenth century. The show is based on Helen Hunt Jackson's classic 1884 romantic novel *Ramona*. Jackson visited San Diego's historic Rancho Guajome Adobe and many claim she based her book on the historic ranch and elegant home.

The Domenigoni Reservoir area includes a 4,500-acre lake, the largest body of water in southern California, 269 billion gallons of water, and 22,000 acres of recreation and open space.

The Maze Stone is a large rock painted with Native American petroglyphs in the style commonly referred to as a maze. Many petroglyphs and pictographs can be found in the hills surrounding Hemet.

Fun facts

· Most of the world's sea gulls are born in California.

· On an annual basis, the gray whale migrates farther than any other mammal. The 12,000-mile round-trip trek includes travel along the entire California coastline.

· With the exception of Alaska, California is home to the most sea otters.

· Fishing from any of California's piers is free and requires no Department of Fish and Game license or permit.

Highland Park

The Southwest Museum, founded in 1907, houses more than 500,000 Native American artifacts. It is considered one of the most important repositories of Native American art in the world.

Hollywood

Hollywood was originally a small planned residential community established by Horace Wilcox. Even though no holly grew there, Wilcox's wife, Daeida, named the town after the home of a woman she met on a train.

The famous Hollywood sign was built in 1923 and read Hollywoodland. It was constructed as a publicity ploy to promote sales of homes in a subdivision by the same name along Beachwood Canyon. In 1949 the Hollywood Chamber of

ROBERT HOLMES/CALTOUR

Handprints, footprints, and messages in the cement in front of Mann's Chinese Theater.

Commerce entered into a contract with the Department of Recreation to repair, rebuild, and to remove the "land" from the sign so it would read "Hollywood." The sign now stretches 450 feet across the side of Mount Lee. It weighs 450,000 pounds.

Squaw Man, directed by Cecil B. DeMille, was the first full-length western movie released in the Hollywood area.

Orson Wells's *Citizen Kane* opened at the El Capital theater in 1939.

On October 18, 1922, the Egyptian Theater, now known as American Cinematheque, hosted the first Hollywood movie premier. The film was *Robin Hood* starring Douglas Fairbanks. Newspaper advertisements heralded "every star and director in the motion picture industry will be there to see the premier." Tickets sold for $5.00.

There is a city law on the books not allowing more than 2,000 sheep to be driven down Hollywood Boulevard at one time.

The first Academy Awards program was held at the Hollywood Roosevelt Hotel in 1929.

The Hollywood Bowl is the world's largest outdoor amphitheater.

The popular tradition of recording footprints, handprints, messages, and signatures of Hollywood notables began in the forecourt of Graumans Chinese Theatre in 1927 when actress Norma Talmadge accidentally stepped into wet cement. The first stars to officially get their footprints in cement at the movie theater were Mary Pickford and Douglas Fairbanks. Graumans Chinese Theatre is now called Mann's Chinese Theater.

The Capital Records building is the world's largest corporate center shaped in the form of the company's product. The building is round to emulate a stack of 45 r.p.m. records, complete with a giant stylus on top. The tower was built in 1956. The lights atop the building spell out "Hollywood" in Morse code.

The first actor to personally receive a star on the Walk of Fame was Joanne Woodward in 1960. On December 17, 1999, actress Sigourney Weaver received the last star placed on the walk in the twentieth century.

Hoopa Valley

The valley contains California's largest Indian reservation.

Humboldt Bay

M.V. Madaket is the oldest passenger-carrying commercial vessel in the country. The historic 1910 ferry has been designated a State Historic Vessel and offers daily cruises from Humboldt Bay.

Humboldt Bay produces and harvests 90 percent of the oysters in the world. During the Arcata Bay Oyster Festival in June, local seafood delicacies, including cracked Dungeness crab, King Salmon, and oysters, are served.

Humboldt County

Reportedly, some of Humboldt County's Victorian buildings are haunted. Ghosts include a female who likes to play 1930s jazz on an antique phonograph, two mischievous children who playfully run through the halls at night, and a ghost named Frank who likes to follow women into the bathroom and then disappear when they see him.

Huntington Beach

Spanning 1,853 feet, the Huntington Beach Pier is the longest concrete municipal pier in the nation. The pier was home to the first surfing contests held in the United States.

Known as Surf City, USA since the popular Jan and Dean song climbed the musical charts, the beach city hosts the International

Surfing Museum and the U.S. Open of Surfing as well as amateur and professional surfing events.

I

Idyllwild

San Jacinto State Park recorded a temperature of 12 degrees below zero in the early 1970s. So far that makes it the coldest California state park. The park also boasts the highest point in the California state parks system with its summit of 10,804 feet.

Imperial Beach

The largest invitational sand castle contest in the nation, the U.S. Open Sand Castle Competition, takes place annually in Imperial Beach in July.

Imperial County

The Algodones Sand Dunes cover 1,000 square miles, making the dune complex one of the largest in North America.

Fun facts

State Flower: Golden Poppy

The Golden Poppy is found thriving in some parts of the state throughout the year. It is found in abundance in a variety of locations and can often be seen scattered along hills and freeways in the state.

Clapp Springs and its palm tree oasis are unique to Palo Verde Mountains Wilderness.

The Indian Pass Wilderness is a distinctive part of the Chocolate Mountains. The region's proximity to the Colorado River and the Arizona desert contribute to the fact that wildlife species not commonly found in the California desert live in the area.

Imperial County has more geothermal energy sites than anywhere else in the United States.

The region is one of the most important flyway corridors for migrant waterfowl, shorebirds, and songbirds in the United States.

Independence

Manzanar, located about 5 miles outside Independence, was the first relocation camp for Japanese Americans. It offers a sobering look at one of ten United States internment centers created at the beginning of World War II. Manzanar War Relocation Center is identified as offering the best opportunities among the ten sites for interpretation of the World War II relocation program.

Indio

More than 95 percent of the dates in the country are produced all

Fun facts

- California is the birthplace of the following food chains: A&W, McDonalds, Dennys, In-N-Out Burger, Carls Jr., Taco Bell, Bob's Big Boy, Del Taco, Winchell's Donuts, Marie Calenders, and Wienerschnitzel.

around Indio. Known as the "Date Capital of the World," Indio hosts the National Date Festival, which is held annually in February.

Ione

The Community Methodist Church of Ione served as the first church in the area. Its cornerstone was laid in 1862 and the structure was completed in 1866. A plaque now recognizes the church, popularly known as the Cathedral of the Mother Lode, as California Historical Landmark #506.

J

Jackson

In the late 1850s Kennedy Mine served as one of the richest gold

Carol Tinneyr

Kennedy Mine Head Frame.

mines in the world and the deepest mine in North America. The mine's headframe stands 125 feet tall. The mine produced more than $34 million in gold.

Jamestown

In 1848 "Gumption," as this town is sometimes called, was a place miners passed through to get to the gold fields. The flow of traffic reversed in a hurry when a gold mass weighing 150 pounds was found at Woods Creek on the edge of town. The Sierra Railway came to Jamestown in 1897 and still operates. Steam engines are rebuilt and maintained at its six-track roundhouse. Railtown 1897 State Historic Park offers a plethora of rolling stock and railroad memorabilia.

Johnsonville

The annual World Championship Longboard Ski Races include the only authentic longboard racing in the world. The Johnsonville site claims to be the oldest recorded ski racing area in the western hemisphere.

Joshua Tree

Giant Rock, located north of Joshua Tree National Park, stands as the world's largest solitary boulder. It is 7 stories high and weighs more than 23,000 tons.

Fun facts

State Fossil: The Saber-toothed Cat

The fossilized remains of this meat-eating cat are found in abundance in Los Angeles at the Rancho La Brea tarpits.

The Joshua tree received its name from early Mormon settlers who thought the large plants looked like the biblical Joshua with his arms extended to heaven.

Julian

More than 260 tons of apples are used in pies each year by the Julian Pie Company, located in this tiny community. In addition, the area is an apple-picker's paradise, with numerous farms and orchards where individuals can select, pick, and pack apples for personal use.

K

Keddie

Keddie is home to the only railroad wye in the world with two legs on bridges and the closing track in a tunnel.

Kelseyville

The "Pear Capital of the World" holds an annual Pear Festival in October.

Kern County

The county is recognized as the number one oil-producing region in the nation.

Kern County Museum and its 16 acres focusing on Kern County's past contain 50 historic buildings and more than 250,000 artifacts. Among the historic buildings are a doctor's office, 1868 log cabin, 1810 Fellows Hotel, Calloway Ranch blacksmith shop, and a one-room schoolhouse.

Kern River Preserve features a riparian forest that includes the state's largest remaining stand of cottonwood and willow trees.

Kernville

What was originally the town of Kernville now lies beneath the waters of Lake Isabella. Several of the town's original buildings were moved to the city's current location on higher ground. Early in its history the town was known as "Whiskey Flat." Today the Whiskey Flat Festival is an annual celebration.

Kingsburg

The citizens of this Swedish village have a water tower made to look like a decorated Scandinavian coffee pot that is 500 times larger than life. It can easily be seen from California Highway 99. It is one of California's favorite welcoming signs.

ROBERT HOLMES/CALTOUR

Kingsburg Water Tower.

Klamath

The Klamath Jet Boat Race is considered the longest of all races of its type. It is held on a whopping 90-mile round-trip course. The first 35 miles provide a flat, twisting, full-throttle run including the intimidating Coon Creek falls area; the course ends with 10 bumpy, rock-strewn miles.

Knight's Ferry

Knight's Ferry Bridge prevails as the longest covered bridge west of the Mississippi.

L

La Canada Flintridge

Descanso Gardens features North America's largest collection of camellias. The gardens cover 165 acres and include a Japanese teahouse.

Fun facts

State Gemstone: Benitoite

The spectacular sapphire-blue gemstone is found in gem quality crystals at only one site in the world: a small deposit in a remote area of the Diablo range in San Benito. The gemstone is one of the world's rarest and most impressive gems.

Laguna Beach

Begun in 1920, the Laguna Playhouse is the oldest continuously operating theater company on the West Coast.

Founded in 1918, the Laguna Art Museum is the oldest art museum in California.

La Jolla

Scripps Institution of Oceanography holds the largest oceanographic museum in the United States. It houses the country's most extensive collection of captive seahorses.

Lake City

Lake City is a city of firsts. The area boasts Modoc County's first organized community, first sawmill, first gristmill, first white man's dwelling, first school, and first wedding. The first gristmill, built in 1869, still stands. Wagon tracks from an emigrant trail can still be seen in nearby places.

Lake Tahoe

Author Mark Twain wrote the lake is "surely the fairest picture the whole earth affords."

The Squaw Valley Olympics were held at Lake Tahoe in 1960. The event introduced a number of firsts, including the first time the

Fun facts

· California state parks annually receive more visitors than the parks in any other state.

Olympics were televised, the first time the cross-country trails were groomed, the first women's 10K relay, and the first time the biathlon was a medal event.

One of the most photographed lakes in the world, Emerald Lake is the largest alpine lake in North America. The body of water stretches 12 miles wide, 22 miles long, and has 72 miles of shoreline.

Lake Tahoe has the largest concentration of skiing resorts in North America. There are 15 downhill and 10 cross-country ski resorts in the area.

Lake Tahoe is the second deepest lake in the United States. It has an average depth of 989 feet with its deepest point being 1,645 feet. The lake contains 39 trillion gallons of water. The water from Lake Tahoe would cover the entire state of California to a depth of 14.5 inches.

Lakewood

In 1953 people hit the California highways in record numbers. In Lakewood the first roadside Denny's Restaurant welcomed travelers. Now a popular chain, the restaurant is known throughout the country for its family fare.

Fun facts

- California was the site of the first radio broadcast.
- California is home to approximately 300,000 Native Americans and 250 different tribes—more than any other state.

Lancaster

The best place to view seasonal poppies, California's official state flower, is the Antelope Valley California Poppy Reserve located west of town.

Saddleback Butte State Park was created to preserve some of the oldest and largest Joshua trees in the world.

Lassen County

Eagle Lake, at 42 square miles, is the second largest natural lake located entirely within California. It is home to the famous and unique Eagle Lake trout.

Westwood mill, the former home of the Red River Lumber Company, operated from 1913 to 1956 and was the largest pine lumber mill in the world at the time.

Le Grand

The oldest steam tractor in North America, dating back to 1893, can be found at Bright's Museum.

Lee Vining

Leroy Vining came to California from Indiana in 1852 and operated a sawmill on the creek near the present-day location of the town. The town is named for this early pioneer.

Eighty-five percent of the California gull population nests in the spring at Mono Lake Tufa State Reserve. The brine fly and brine shrimp, found only in Mono Lake, are a major source of food for tens of thousands of birds migrating to the area annually.

Leggett

Between Leggett and the north coast, Sinkyone Wilderness State Park provides an isolated area 230 feet below sea level. It is the only state park to use the word "wilderness" in its name and serves as the lowest point in the California state parks system. The park can also be entered through the Garberville area.

Lindsay

In the 1880s Julius Orton planted the first of many orange trees in the area, giving rise to the moniker "Central California's Citrus Center."

For many years the community was recognized as the "Olive Capital of the World" and served as the home of the Lindsay Olive Company's main office and plant. The olive company is no more. The 6-foot-diameter concrete pitted black olive that once decorated the plant has been moved to the Olive Tree Inn.

Fun facts

- California leads the United States in crop and livestock commodity production.
- Almonds, artichokes, dates, figs, kiwi fruit, olives, pistachios, pomegranates, prunes, raisins, and walnuts are all American crops grown exclusively in California, making California the nation's leading agricultural state.
- Were California a separate country it would rank among the top eight economies in the world.

Little River

When actor James Dean stayed in Little River during the filming of *East of Eden*, he was ordered out of the dining room of a local inn for putting his feet on the table.

The rooms where Alan Alda and Ellen Burstyn cuddled in the film *Same Time, Next Year* remain popular with couples staying at the Heritage House.

Livermore

Wente Winery is the oldest continuously operating family-owned winery in California.

The local Stockman's Association hosts the annual "World's Fastest Rodeo." The slogan and name were first used in 1935 because the short turnaround time between events and contestants makes this rodeo fast, fun, rapid-fire excitement.

Locke

The town was constructed entirely by and for the Chinese whose ancestors were early California settlers.

Lomita

The Lomita Railroad Museum, the first of its kind west of Colorado, focuses on the era of the steam locomotive.

Lompoc

La Purisima Conception is considered to be California's best example of mission architecture. Plants were brought from other mission gardens to form one of the finest collections of early California flora in existence. In California, the year 1812 was known as "El año de los temblores," or "The year of the earthquakes." A major earthquake struck La Purisima on December 21, 1812, destroying many of the mission's structures.

There is a city law on the books forbidding the possession, ownership, or raising of roosters because they disturb the peace.

Lone Pine

Alabama Hills Recreation Lands serves as a mecca for movie buffs. A plaque at the corner of Whitney Portal Road and Movie Road tells the tale. Since the 1920s the rugged hills have served as sites for films such as *How the West Was Won, Maverick, The Shadow, Bengal Lancers,* and the television series *Bonanza; Have Gun, Will Travel;* and *Death Valley Days.* A local mountain road provided the site where Lucy and Desi drove their trailer in the 1954 film *The Long, Long Trailer.*

Dozens of actors in town to film movies and television productions have carved their names in the walls and front door frame of the Indian Trading Post on Main Street.

In 1872 the Owens Valley was hit by an earthquake measuring 8.3 on the Richter scale. Twenty-seven people were killed in this disaster

Fun facts

State Marine Mammal: California Gray Whale

The majestic California Gray Whale measures 30 to 50 feet in length and weighs up to 40 tons. Each year the whales embark on a 12,000-mile migration from the Arctic to the lagoons of Baja California and back. The migrations generally occur between December and April. The whales can be seen at various locations throughout the coastal regions of the state.

that nearly destroyed Lone Pine. On a hill overlooking the valley, a common grave for 16 of the victims provides a memorial of the devastating quake.

The railroad depot located about 2 miles north of town is one of the few Southern Pacific railroad depot buildings still remaining in the state.

Long Beach

Boasting 400 handles of beer, The Yard House restaurant, located at Shoreline Village, serves the world's largest number of beers on tap.

The world's largest mural, *Planet Ocean*, can be found in the Long Beach Arena. Images of water, whales, and other sea life cover the 116,000-square-foot exterior wall of the circular arena.

The Aquarium of the Pacific is the only aquarium in the United States to focus on the entire Pacific Ocean. The following regions are included in the exhibits and displays: Southern California/Baja; Northern Pacific; and the Tropical Pacific.

The fictional three-hour tour to *Gilligan's Island* began on the S.S. *Minnow*, a cabin cruiser that sailed from Long Beach's Alamitos Bay in 1964.

In 1908 Long Beach revolutionized the lifeguard industry by becoming the first city in California with an organized lifeguard service.

The nation's narrowest privately owned home, the Skinny House, was built in 1932. It was constructed on a bet that the builder could not build a habitable residence on a lot that measured only 10 by 50 feet. The house is three stories high, contains 860 square feet, and is built in the Old English Tudor style.

Bert Grimm's Tattoo Studio is the nation's oldest tattoo parlor still in business today.

The city has the largest Cambodian population outside the country of Cambodia. Approximately 40,000 Cambodians live in the area.

Long Beach was the first tinseltown. Balboa Studios was based in Long Beach and attracted silent film stars like Fatty Arbuckle and Theda Bara. Other celebrities who frequented the seaside community included W. C. Fields, Clark Gable, and Carol Lombard.

The Marine Stadium, built in 1932 for an Olympic rowing competition, was the first manmade rowing course in the United States and the first in the world designed specifically for rowing and boating.

Firefighters Museum houses all types of vintage firefighting paraphernalia including photographs of Sam, the harbor station's cat immortalized in a Little Golden Book story for his passion for sliding down a fire pole.

The *Queen Mary* was the most luxurious liner ever built. She embarked on her maiden voyage from Southampton in 1936. She was conscripted into service in 1939 when she became a troopship capable of transporting 5,000 soldiers at a time. The historic ship made her permanent home in Long Beach in 1967.

In 1911 aviator Cal Rodgers completed the first transcontinental air flight by landing in Long Beach. In 1912 Horace Kearney used Long Beach as a starting point for the world's first passenger flight.

More than 200,000 racing fans flock to Long Beach each year to witness the Toyota Grand Prix, the nation's biggest race through city streets.

Los Angeles

The diverse multiethnic population distinguishes the city as the cultural hub of the Pacific Rim. People from about 140 countries, speaking approximately 96 different languages, call the region home. Los Angeles has the largest Asian/Pacific Island population and contains the fourth-largest African American metropolitan area population in the United States.

Los Angeles Harbor is one of the largest deepwater ports in the United States.

Just off the coast near Los Angeles Harbor lies the southwestern tip of the North American continent. It is marked by the sky tower at Long Point.

The manmade rock jetty at Los Angeles Harbor is the longest breakwater in the world.

Angeles Gate/Los Angeles Harbor Lighthouse is the only lighthouse in the world that emits an emerald-colored beacon.

Loyola University was the first institution of higher learning in southern California.

Autry Museum of Western Heritage is the only museum in the nation that depicts the history of the American West from prehistoric times to the present.

The Carole & Barry Kaye Museum of Miniatures contains the largest collection of miniatures in the world. Diminutive mansions, pint-sized automobiles, and small decorated rooms are some of the undersized exhibits.

Avila Adobe, the city's oldest existing house, was built in 1818.

More university graduates per capita live in Los Angeles than any other United States city.

Topanga State Park, containing more than 11,000 acres, provides the largest wilderness area within a city's limits in the world.

More artists, writers, filmmakers, actors, dancers, and musicians live and work in Los Angeles than in any other city in the history of civilization.

The city has the largest number of women-owned businesses in the nation.

Located in downtown Los Angeles, Angels Flight, the shortest railway in the world, opened in 1901. It was restored in 1995 and rededicated in 1996. Two original train cars travel the less-than-300-foot incline quickly and easily.

Los Angeles is the only city in the world divided in two by a mountain range—the Santa Monica Mountains. It is also the only city divided by a national recreation area—the Santa Monica Mountains National Recreation Area.

The annual California International Antiquarian Book Fair is billed as the world's largest rare book fair in the world. It is sanctioned by the Antiquarian Booksellers Association of America.

Los Angeles Convention & Visitors Bureau

Angels Flight.

Items found at the fair include early printed books and manuscripts, illustrated books, fine bindings, early American literature, and much more. It is held alternately in Los Angeles and San Francisco.

Longitudinally, the city lies farther east than Reno, Nevada.

The Los Angeles Flower District holds the distinction of being the largest single flower district in the United States. In addition to plants and flowers, the facility features the largest array of floral supplies on the West Coast.

Hollyhock House was the first Frank Lloyd Wright residence constructed in Los Angeles. The house is located in Barnsdall Park and is open for tours.

Tail 'the Cock restaurant introduced the margarita cocktail to the public in 1955.

The hot fudge sundae became famous at C. C. Brown's restaurant in 1906.

Santa Monica Mountains National Recreation Area stretches west from Los Angeles to the Ventura County line and from Point Mugu to Santa Monica along the California shoreline. The area contains 150,000 acres and is the country's largest urban unit of the national park system. One in every seventeen Americans lives within one hour's drive of this recreation area. The area has more area codes and zip codes than any unit in the national park system.

Fortune cookies got their start in Los Angeles in 1916.

The Japanese American National Museum is the only museum in the United States dedicated to sharing the experiences of Americans of Japanese ancestry.

The city is home to Mattel Inc., the world's largest toy manufacturer and Barbie creator; the first passenger airline in the world;

the first supermarket; the first B2 Bomber; and the first F11-7 Stealth Fighter.

There have been many automobile-related developments in Los Angeles including the first gas station, the first freeway, and the first parking meter.

Griffith Park, encompassing more than 4,000 acres of land, is the largest city-run park in the country. The park includes the Los Angeles Zoo, Griffith Observatory, Travel Town, a carousel, pony and train rides, and more than 50 miles of bridle and hiking trails.

Travel Town contains the largest collection of steam locomotives west of the Mississippi River.

The use of the "doggie bag" began at Lawry's restaurant in 1938.

Los Angeles contains more museums per capita than any other city in the nation, more stage productions than in any other American metropolitan region, and more resident artists than any other city in the world.

Los Angeles is the only location in the world to twice host the Summer Olympics.

The largest historical theater district listed on the National Register of Historic Places features nickelodeons, vaudeville houses, theaters, and movie palaces. The district runs along Broadway between Third and Ninth Streets.

Fun facts

- California has a total of 24 volcanoes, including Mount Lassen, Mount Shasta, and Mount Mammoth.
- California has 1.3 million acres designated as state parks.

California Mart, covering 3 million square feet, is the largest apparel wholesale market in the world.

Los Angeles County

The Los Angeles County Museum of Art is the largest art museum west of the Mississippi River. It houses a collection of more than 500,000 works dating from ancient times to the present.

Los Angeles County has the largest Hispanic population in the United States. Only Mexico City and Guadalajara have larger Hispanic populations.

Hidden away in the northern part of the county, Arthur B. Ripley Desert Woodland State Park contains one of the Antelope Valley's last virgin juniper and Joshua tree forests. A roadside directional sign identifies the location of the park. Its only visitor amenity is a rustic outhouse.

The Los Angeles County Fair's hometown is Pomona.

> The first fair ran from October 17 to 21, 1922. Admission was 50 cents a day.
>
> Demonstrations on how to make toothpaste from orange by-products were popular attractions at the 1922 fair.
>
> The fair crowned its first queen in 1929. Her name was Edna Mae Paige.
>
> On September 19, 1932, California Governor James Rolph Jr., attended the fair and dedicated a new horseracing grandstand. It is said he had to run for his life when a team of six horses came running around the corner, heading his way. The governor sprinted 50 yards to safety, beating some of the fastest horses at their own game.
>
> Wedding bells rang at the fair for the first time in 1933 when cowboy actor Monty Montana wed Louise Archer in front of the racetrack

grandstand. Montana waited at the altar on his trusted pinto Comanche Spot. Archer rode to the altar on Lady Spot.

Fair visitors purchased and presumably consumed three tons of popcorn costing $720,000 in 1938. In addition 18,000 hot dogs and 24,000 hamburgers were eaten.

During World War II the fair did not operate. On March 26, 1942, the army took over the entire fairgrounds except the administration building.

The fair adopted Thummer the pig as its official mascot in 1948. The pig's name comes from the fact that one of its outstretched hoofs made him appear to be hitchhiking his way to the fair.

The popular "Hot Dog on a Stick" debuted at the 1948 fair.

In 1957, for the first time at any fair, the Ringling Bros. and Barnum and Bailey Circus was a major feature.

The world's largest ski jump made with artificial snow was billed as one of the main attractions at the 1960 fair. The jump was 300 feet long and rose 130 feet in the air.

In 1972 fair visitors consumed 40 tons of hot dogs, 1 million tortillas, and 15 tons of hamburgers.

The Los Angeles County Fair's annual attendance figures make it the largest county fair in North America.

Each year more than 100,000 people have their feet massaged on Footsie Wootsie machines during the fair.

During a typical fair run, 1.5 million pounds of ice are used.

Los Banos

The San Luis Reservoir State Recreation Area west of town, with its 2,041 acre-feet capacity, operates as the largest off-stream reservoir anywhere in the world.

Los Osos

California oaks estimated to be 700 years old may be viewed at the 85-acre Los Osos Oaks Reserve, home of several species of lichen found nowhere else in the world. Wisps of lichens and mosses dangle from oak branches throughout the reserve.

M

Malibu

In 1960 the world's first laser was successfully operated by its inventor, Theodore Maiman, at Hughes Research Laboratories.

Manhattan Beach

Although battered by storms and ocean currents, the Manhattan Beach Pier prevails as the oldest remaining example of reinforced concrete pier construction in southern California.

Manteca

The riparian brush rabbit calls Caswell Memorial State Park home. Endemic only to the California state parks system, the

Fun facts

State Mineral: Native Gold

California has produced more gold than any other state in the nation. The mineral can still be found in streambeds and can be panned at several locations in the state.

critter lives in approximately 255 acres of the area's once-vast hardwood forest.

Maricopa

A Union Oil Company well in Maricopa produced 9 million barrels of oil in 18 months. It is considered America's most spectacular gusher.

Marin County

Marin County Civic Center is prominent as the last and one of the most important works designed by the internationally acclaimed architect Frank Lloyd Wright. The center is a national and state historical landmark. Wright died April 9, 1959, at the age of 92, and didn't see the building completed. The civic center is featured prominently in the film *Gattaca*.

Marin County reportedly has the largest concentration of hot tubs and BMW automobiles in the country.

Basic Instinct, starring Sharon Stone, brought coastal Marin to the big screen.

The Pacific Coast's highest concentration of hawks soar in the Tennessee Valley.

Marina del Rey

Brimming with thousands of pleasure crafts and abundant dockage, Marina del Rey serves as the world's largest manmade recreational harbor.

Mariposa

The *Mariposa Gazette* is California's oldest weekly newspaper in continuous publication. It has not missed an issue since January

1854. The Mariposa Museum and History Center houses the newspaper's original press and print shop.

The highest known grade of crystalline gold continues to be mined in Mariposa.

Mariposa County

El Capitan, the largest rock monolith in the country, stands 3,593 feet tall.

The three tallest waterfalls in North America can be found in Mariposa County: Yosemite Falls (2,425 feet); Sentinel Falls (2,000 feet); and Ribbon Falls (1,612 feet).

The highest pass in the Sierra Nevada Mountains is Tioga Pass at 9,945 feet above sea level.

Opened in 1854, the Mariposa County Court House is the oldest county courthouse in continuous use west of the Rocky Mountains.

Mariposa County is the largest county in the state containing no stop lights.

Mariposa County is the only county with a mineral (Mariposite) and a flower (Mariposa lily) named after it.

Mariposa is the only county named for an insect. In Spanish the word "mariposa" means butterfly.

California's original ski area, located at Badger Pass, is still in use.

Wawona Covered Bridge in Yosemite National Park is the only covered bridge in the United States national parks system. At an elevation of 4,000 feet above sea level, the bridge is also the highest covered bridge in the nation. Built in 1878, the bridge crosses the south fork of the Merced River and leads to an 1880s pioneer village.

Martinez

Baseball player Joe DiMaggio was born in Martinez.

McKinleyville

The tallest totem pole in the United States is 160 feet tall, weighs 57,000 pounds, made of painted and carved wood, and located in McKinleyville. The totem pole was carved from a 500-year-old redwood tree.

Mendocino

In Mendocino historic water towers still survive tucked among old sea captains' homes, shops, inns, and restaurants. The town's oldest tower was built in 1857.

Millions of television viewers believed star Angela Lansbury spent time on location in Maine. However, *Murder She Wrote's* Cabot Cove was in fact the town of Mendocino in disguise.

Cape Mendocino is the westernmost point in the continental United States.

Mentryville

The oil well known as Pico No. 4 was the longest continually operating oil well in the world at the time of its closure. It was capped in September 1990.

Mill Valley

Muir Woods National Monument's Cathedral and Bohemian Grove contains the park's largest redwoods. The tallest is 252 feet and the thickest is nearly 14 feet across. Muir Woods is one of the San Francisco Bay area's last uncut stands of old-growth redwood trees.

Mission Hills

Mission San Fernando, built in 1797, is the largest freestanding adobe building in the United States. The mission has 4-foot-thick adobe brick walls. The structure originally was used as a hospice for travelers.

Mokelumne Hill

On the northeast corner of Main and Church Streets stands the oldest Congregational Church building in the state. It was erected on August 28, 1953.

Modesto

The Modesto Arch spans Ninth and I Streets and includes the name of the city and the slogan, "Water, Wealth, Contentment, Health." Arches were once extremely popular in cities across the country. Today the arch in Modesto is one of the few still remaining in California.

Modesto Junior College, established in 1921, was the first junior college in the state.

The popular film *American Graffiti* was based on producer George Lucas's boyhood experiences in Modesto.

Fun facts

· In 1855 Secretary of War Jefferson Davis learned of a plan to import camels to serve on a mail and supply wagon route between California and Texas. It was thought that one day every mail route across the continent would be worked by camels. When the Civil War began, the Camel Military Corps' efforts declined and eventually ended.

Carhops at the A&W Rootbeer Drive-In still cruise out to the cars on roller skates.

Two Modesto companies serve as the world's largest: E. & J. Gallo Winery is the largest winery and Tri-Valley Growers is the largest cannery.

Modoc County

The county museum, located in Alturas, contains perhaps the most complete collection of Indian arts, pioneer guns, and other early settler articles found anywhere in the nation.

Fur trappers were led to the area in 1832 and are the first documented non-Indian people to stay in Modoc County.

Cedar Pass Ski Hill is the northeasternmost ski area in California equipped with a chair lift.

Mojave Desert

Twenty-five miles north of town, Red Rock Canyon State Park seems to be a favorite site for filmmakers. The beginning sequence in *Jurassic Park* was filmed in the park and the canyon is often used as a location for western and science fiction films, commercials, and documentaries.

A lone telephone still stands in the Mojave National Preserve. Reportedly installed long ago when nearby miners used it, the isolated desert phone had push buttons installed in the 1970s. The still-working phone suffers from frequent vandalism but is available for anyone to use.

Monterey

California's first and last American consul's residence is the

Thomas O. Larkin home located in Monterey State Historic Park. Larkin was posted to California in 1844.

Colton Hall, now a museum, was the site of the signing of California's first constitution in 1849.

The Monterey Jazz Festival bills itself as the oldest event of its kind in the world.

Although the sardines are long gone, in the 1940s Cannery Row was known as the "Sardine Capital of the World." Better known, perhaps, are John Steinbeck's novels *Cannery Row* and *Sweet Thursday,* both of which immortalized Cannery Row.

Cannery Row was rated the number one shore-access scuba diving area in the United States by *Rodale Scuba* magazine.

California's First Theatre was launched by United States soldiers in 1850. Performances continue in the facility throughout the year.

Located on Monterey Bay, Point Pinos Lighthouse is the state's oldest lighthouse in continuous operation.

Don Juan Cabrillo, a Portuguese explorer, gets credit for being the first of the Spanish explorers to anchor in Monterey Bay. He sailed into the area in 1542. In 1602 Sebastian Vizcaino became the first European to set foot on the Monterey Peninsula.

The undersea Monterey Canyon is the largest submarine canyon on the West Coast.

Monterey Bay Aquarium's hometown is Monterey.

AstroTurf keeps the octopuses from escaping their exhibits. It is the only material their suction cups can't grab onto.

Foam torpedoes called "pigs" are used to clean marine life out of the aquarium's seawater pipes. Unless the pipes are "pigged" regularly, they become clogged with animals that grow inside the pipes.

Shorebirds in the Sandy Shore Aviary maintain a diet of meal-worms, crickets, and other food.

It costs $200,000 per year to feed the aquarium's more than 300,000 sea creatures.

Sevengill sharks are coaxed to eat vitamin-enriched salmon steaks clipped to the end of a long pole and waved in front of their faces as they swim by.

The aquarium features the first living kelp forest ever created outside the wild. At 28 feet tall, the kelp forest is one of the tallest aquarium exhibits in the world.

The acrylic window at the Outer Bay exhibit is the largest aquarium window in the world. It is 17 x 56 1/2 feet and 13 inches thick.

The aquarium contains the largest jellyfish galleries in the world.

Mountain Ranch

California Caverns is a major cavern system; it was first written about in 1850, making it one of the earliest officially recorded caves in the Mother Lode region of California.

Rob Lewine/Photographer

Monterey Bay Aquarium.

Morro Bay

The town's namesake, Morro Rock, was the last to develop of a chain of nine volcanic peaks stretching from Morro Bay to San Luis Obispo. Sometimes called the "Gibraltar of the Pacific," Morro Rock has served as an important navigational landmark for more than 300 years.

The Morro Bay kangaroo rat survives exclusively on less than 400 acres of land located at the southeast end of the bay.

Tiny Anchor Memorial Park is dedicated to anglers from around the world who have been lost at sea. The names of the lost continue to be added as sea tragedies occur. Names are engraved on a memorial featuring a 7,000-pound anchor forged in 1830.

Morro Bay Giant Chessboard measures 16 feet square. The chess pieces are made of redwood carved from salvaged wood from old water tanks. Each of the pieces weighs up to 20 pounds. The pawns stand 22 inches high, the kings are 33 inches tall, and the queens measure in at 31 inches. Normal-sized chess enthusiasts regularly play the game with the giant-sized pieces.

Heron's nests can be viewed at the Heron Rookery State Reserve. The rookery is considered the most significant great blue heron nesting site between San Francisco and the Mexican border. Herons nest in the area's tall eucalyptus trees between February and July.

Mount Shasta City

Mount Shasta City features the oldest working fish hatchery in California.

Murphys

One of the oldest hotels still operating in the state is Murphys Hotel. The old hotel register includes the names of Mark Twain, Horatio Alger, Ulysses S. Grant, and Charles Bolton, also known as Black Bart.

The bandit Joaquin Murieta is said to have begun his murderous career in Murphys. What was claimed to be the preserved head of Murieta was later displayed at numerous locations around the state.

N

Needles

The town was named for the pinnacles of the nearby Black Mountains, which are actually located in Arizona but visible from California.

Peanuts fans, who for many years cherished the Charles Schulz cartoon and its cast of characters, recognize Needles as the fictional hometown of Spike, the brother of Snoopy.

Fun facts

State Motto: Eureka!

The motto is Greek, meaning "I have found it." The saying refers to the great discovery of gold in 1848.

Nevada City

Built in 1860 with handhewn local timber, the Oregon Creek bridge stands as the oldest covered bridge in California. Locals boldly boast it is also the only covered bridge in the United States installed backward. After it was washed away by a flood, a team of oxen towed it back to a convenient crossing, and it was reinstalled backward.

The Nevada Theatre is the oldest building in the state erected as a theater. It is still in use today.

President Herbert Hoover lived and worked as a gold miner in Nevada City.

New Almaden

The New Almaden Quicksilver Mine is considered the oldest, richest, and most productive mine in California and North America. Discovered in November 1845 by Captain Andre Castillero, it preceded the historic Sutter's Mill gold discovery of January 1848.

Newhall

Contrary to what some people think, the first discovery of gold in California didn't occur at Sutter's Mill but six years earlier in the Santa Clarita Valley near Newhall. The Oak of the Golden Dream commemorates the first gold discovery.

Well CSO-4, or Pico No. 4, serves as California's first commercially productive well. It was spudded in 1876 by Demetrious Scofield, who later became the first president of Standard Oil Company of California.

Newport Beach

Newport Beach Harbor is recognized as the largest small boat harbor in the world.

In 1889 a group of enterprising local anglers began the Dory Fishing Fleet. Still located adjacent to the Newport Pier, the open-air market offers fresh seafood. The fleet is the last beachside cooperative of its kind in the United States.

The International Yacht Race, with more than 500 entrants each year, sails in as the largest and one of the oldest races of its kind in the world.

Niles

Long before Hollywood rose to fame, the small burg of Niles served as the first moviemaking capital of the state. In the early 1900s more than 450 movies were made in the area. On the sidewalks around town are painted markers honoring silent movie actors and locations where movies were filmed.

Noyo River Valley

The valley's residents are the only Californians who still receive individual mail delivery service by train. The Skunk Train provides mail service to 18 rural residents 6 days a week year-round. (See Fort Bragg for additional information.)

O

Oak Glen

Oak Glen is famous for its apples. The first apple tree in the area was planted in the late 1860s at Parrish Pioneer Ranch. Oak Glen maintains popular orchards and self-pick apple stands.

The Enoch Parrish home, built in 1876, is the oldest all-timber residence in San Bernardino County.

Oakhurst

Chateau Miel's World of Coffee boasts the world's largest espresso station.

Oakland

The popsicle got its start in Oakland. By accident, in 1905, 11-year-old Frank Epperson froze some soda water and created one of America's favorite sweet treats. According to a legend, the youngster left the liquid on his porch with a stirring stick in it; the temperature dropped below freezing and the famous confection was born.

Lake Merrit was declared America's first state game refuge in 1870. Today it is the only salt water lake located in the heart of a city.

Following a devastating earthquake in 1873, the Alameda County seat was moved to Oakland where it has remained for more than 125 years.

Fun facts

· Actor Ronald Reagan served as governor of California before becoming the fortieth president of the United States.

· California is the number one travel destination in the United States.

· In 1911, 9 years before the rest of the nation, California granted women the right to vote.

The Central Pacific Railroad selected the city as the terminus of the transcontinental railroad, which was completed in 1869 to provide a vital link to the East.

The "human wave," sports fans' synchronized up and down movement in stadiums, was invented in Oakland during the seventh-inning stretch of the final playoff game between the Oakland Athletics and New York Yankees on October 15, 1981. "Crazy George" Henderson was the creator.

Mother's Cake & Cookie Company, the largest cookie producer in the United States, has been located in Oakland since 1914.

Among the famous people born in Oakland are actors Isadora Duncan, Clint Eastwood, Marla Gibbs, and Tom Hanks; authors Bret Harte, Rod McKuen, Joaquin Miller, Gertrude Stein, and Robert Louis Stevenson; musicians Sheila E. Lowell Fulson, John Handy, Earl "Fatha" Hines, the Pointer Sisters, and Tower of Power; politicians Edwin Meese, Jr., and Earl Warren; and sport figures Reggie Jackson, Ernie Lombardi, Gary Pettis, Casey Stengel, Bill Russell, John Brodie, MacArthur Land, Buster Crabbe, Don Budge, James Robinson, and Archie Williams.

Fun facts

State Nickname: The Golden State

The nickname is highly appropriate. It refers to California's development and remarkable prosperity which began with the discovery of gold.

Oceano

Oceano Dunes State Vehicular Recreation Area and MacKerricher State Park in Cleone both feature the state's most extensive sand dunes located in the California state parks system.

Oceanside

Historic, scenic Highway 101, a major thoroughfare running the full length of the state, began in Oceanside when wagons and primitive autos competed for space on its narrow, bumpy, unpredictable dirt surface. The highway is often called the "coast road" since it follows the coastline in many areas of the state.

Oceanside Pier extends more than a quarter mile, making it one of the longest wooden piers on the West Coast. The nearby California Surf Museum focuses on the history and lure of one of California's most popular sports and lifestyles.

Mission San Luis Rey, known as the "king of missions," is the largest mission in California. The mission blends Mexican, Moorish, and

CalTour/Robert Holmes

Scenic Hwy 1 follows the California shoreline in places the larger, faster Hwy 101 can't.

Spanish architecture. The mission gardens include a fruit orchard where the first pepper tree in California still grows near the Carriage Arch entrance. It was brought by ship from Peru and planted in 1830. The mission was dedicated in 1798 and is the only remaining cross-shaped mission in California.

Olema

Olema is best known for being the spot with the greatest amount of ground movement during the 1906 earthquake that devastated San Francisco.

Ontario

There is a city law on the books making it illegal for a rooster to crow within the city limits.

OCEANSIDE CHAMBER OF COMMERCE

Mission San Luis Rey.

Orick

Orick is known as the Burl Art capital of the world.

Oroville

The town was founded in 1850 as Ophir, a gold rush town once having the largest Chinatown in the state. A reminder of that claim, the Chinese Temple and Garden, a museum of Asian artifacts, was built in 1856. It is listed on the National Register of Historic Places.

The last living Yahi Yana Indian was discovered in an Oroville corral in 1911.

Movies such as *Gone with the Wind* and the original *Robin Hood* were filmed in nearby Bidwell Park.

At 770 feet in height, the Oroville Dam is the tallest earth-filled dam in the United States. It is 6,920 feet long. Clay from the Feather River Valley was the material used to construct the dam.

Lake Oroville was ranked by *Bassmaster Magazine* as the number one bass fishing lake in California.

The Feather River Fish Hatchery accommodates up to 11,000 salmon and trout twice yearly.

Oxnard

The Financial Tower stands as the tallest commercial building between Los Angeles and San Francisco.

Known as the "Strawberry Capital of California," the agricultural town is the largest producer of strawberries in the state and grows half the state's overall volume. The city features an annual California Strawberry Festival.

Pacific Grove

Point Pinos Lighthouse, heralded as the oldest continuously operating lighthouse on the West Coast, is open to the public Thursday through Saturday, 1:00 to 4:00 P.M.

Butterfly Town, USA, each year becomes the home of millions of butterflies, which spend the winter there. Pacific Grove boasts an annual butterfly parade that celebrates the orange and black species known as the monarch.

There is a city law on the books establishing a $500 fine for molesting butterflies.

PACIFIC GROVE CHAMBER OF COMMERCE

Point Pinos Lighthouse.

Palm Desert

The Living Desert is popularly known for its wildlife. It is also home to thousands of plants native to deserts around the world.

One of the wildest shows on wheels, the Palm Desert Golf Cart Parade started as a lark for locals in 1964. The world's only golf cart parade has grown into an annual event including more than 100 decorated carts plus marching bands and celebrities.

Palm Springs

The three canyons containing North America's largest natural fan palm oases—Andreas, Murray, and Palm Canyons—are located on the tribal lands of the Aqua Caliente band of Cauhilla Indians. The oldest palms are estimated to be 1,500 to 2,000 years old.

Some of California's most notorious fault lines, including the world-famous San Andreas Fault, run near the Palm Springs desert resorts. It is possible to walk directly on these fault lines and learn how earthquakes have changed the face of the desert during the last 200 million years.

Singers Frank Sinatra and Ginny Simms; musician and senator Salvatore (Sonny) Bono; songwriters Frederick Lowe and Jimmy Van Heusen; singer/dancer Busby Berkeley; and actors William Powell, Charlie Farrell, and Cameron Mitchell are among the numerous dignitaries buried at Desert Memorial Park.

Palm Springs Aerial Tramway operates as the largest vertical cable ride in the United States and the second largest in the world. The actual length of the cable system itself is 12,800 feet. The ascent takes passengers through five different life zones, from the hot Sonoran desert to a cool alpine wilderness.

Debuted in the year 2000, the Palm Springs Aerial Tramway cars are the largest rotating tram cars in the world. They provide riders a 360-degree view of the scenery as they travel to the top of 6,000-foot Mount San Jacinto.

Fabulous Palm Springs Follies features California's oldest professional chorus line.

The Moorten Botanical Gardens has been in existence for many years. It is a wonderland of more than 2,000 varieties of giant cacti, trees, birds, succulents, and flowers.

With more than 100 golf courses in the desert valley, the Palm Springs area prospers as the "Golf Capital of the World."

PALM SPRINGS TOURISM

Scenic Palm Springs.

Fun facts

State Reptile: The Desert Tortoise

An endangered species, the desert tortoise lives to be 100 to 125 years old and is a California native. It is a contemporary of the wool rhinoceros and the mammoth.

Palmdale

Edwards Air Force Base has the longest runway in the world—7.5 miles.

Palomar Mountain

Hale Telescope at the Palomar Observatory contains a main mirror made of a 14-ton disk of Pyrex glass, the heaviest piece of glass in the world.

ROBERT HOLMES/CALTOUR

Desert Tortoise.

Pasadena

Opened in 1940, the Pasadena Freeway, popularly known as the Arroyo Seco, is considered the Los Angeles area's first freeway.

The Gamble House, once the home of David and Mary Gamble of Proctor & Gamble fame, is the most complete and best preserved example of the work of internationally noted architects Charles and Henry Green. Built in 1908, the mansion features rare woods and original furnishings.

Castle Green was built in 1898 and still contains most of its original interior furnishings. A popular filming site, it can be seen in *Bugsy, Sneakers*, and *The Marrying Man*, and it is where the sting takes place in *The Sting* starring Paul Newman and Robert Redford.

The Beaux Arts–style Fenyes Mansion, now home to the Pasadena Historical Museum, was once owned by the Finnish consul. It offers a glimpse of the extravagant lifestyle that existed on Pasadena's Millionaire's Row at the turn of the century. Scenes from *Newsies, Eleanor and Franklin*, and *Being There* were filmed at the mansion.

Other famous Pasadena homes include the *Batman* mansion, the *Father of the Bride* house, the Drysdale and Clampett estates from the film version of *The Beverly Hillbillies*, and the Carrington Mansion from *Dynasty*.

The Pacific Asia Museum is the only museum in the southwestern United States dedicated to the arts and culture of Asia and the Pacific.

The Wrigley Mansion, once the home of famous chewing-gum manufacturer William Wrigley Jr., today serves as the headquarters for the Pasadena Tournament of Roses Association.

The Tournament of Roses Parade and Rose Bowl Game's hometown is Pasadena.

These two events are the premier New Year's Day celebrations. More than 1 million people line the street for the parade. Many arrive early with sleeping bags and other means for spending time after they seek out the ideal parade viewing location. Nearly 500 million people watch the festivities on television.

The first Tournament of Roses was held in 1890.

Tournament Park became home to the first Tournament East-West Football Game in 1900.

The first Rose Bowl Game was played at Tournament Park in 1902; the University of Michigan defeated Stanford University.

Construction of the horseshoe-shaped Rose Bowl was completed in 1922. The stadium was built in a ravine of parkland and natural vegetation on the west side of town.

The first worldwide shortwave radio broadcast of the Tournament of Roses Parade took place in 1932.

The first Rose Bowl Game was telecast in 1947.

Super Bowl XI was the first Super Bowl played in the Rose Bowl stadium.

ROBERT HOLMES/CALTOUR

Tournament of Roses Parade.

The first live network broadcast in Spanish of the Rose Bowl Game took place in 1988.

The theme of the year 2000 Tournament of Roses Parade and Rose Bowl Game was appropriately "Celebration 2000: Visions of the Future."

Paso Robles

Among the local pioneer artifacts and historical memorabilia found at El Paso de Robles Area Pioneer Museum is the largest assemblage of barbed wire in California. The collection was amassed by local resident Swift Jewel. Barbed wire is considered one of the most important cattle industry inventions.

Well-known Polish pianist Ignace Paderewski first came to Paso Robles in 1913. Later he purchased two local ranches and brought

ROBERT HOLMES/CALTOUR

Lone Cypress.

the first Zinfandel grapes to the area. The town's annual Paderewski Festival celebrates the arts.

Pebble Beach

A scenic landmark, the Lone Cypress tree located on 17-Mile Drive on the Monterey Peninsula is 200 to 300 years old. Cypress trees are a species native only to this region and can live up to 4,000 years.

Petaluma

Petaluma Adobe State Historic Park is home to California's largest secular (non-mission) adobe building. Today, the building consists of approximately 85 percent of the original adobe and 25 percent of the original lumber used in its construction. Visitors can see the method used to construct adobe using earth and straw.

California's oldest continuously operating shoe store was established in 1870 in Petaluma. The store's sliding wall ladders were installed in 1880 and are still used daily.

Filmmakers often use the town as a location for shooting feature films and made-for-television movies and commercials. Films

Fun facts

· California's wineries produce 75 percent of the wine sold in the nation.

· Covering 158,693 square miles, California is the third largest state in the nation. The average width of the state is 150 to 200 miles.

· California's coastline is more than 1,264 miles long.

shot here include *American Graffiti*, *Peggy Sue Got Married*, *Shadow of a Doubt*, *Basic Instinct*, a remake of *Lolita*, and *Phenomenon* with John Travolta.

The first recorded airmail flight in the United States was made by Fred Wiseman from Petaluma to Santa Rosa in 1911.

In 1912 Petaluma's Carlson & Currier silk mill (now Sunset Line & Twine) received the first North American transcontinental truck delivery. The cargo was three tons of Parrot Brand Olive Silk Soap sponsored by the American Locomotive Company, builders of the ALCO truck. The delivery crossed the 4,145 miles of rough roads from Philadelphia to Petaluma in 94 days.

Known as the "World's Egg Basket" since 1918, the city remained tops in egg production until after World War II, shipping millions of eggs by train and steamboat to destinations as far away as Buenos Aires, London, and Paris.

In 1923 the world's only institution for the study and treatment of avian pathology was established when J. E. Keyes opened the Chicken Pharmacy on Main Street. It dispensed 50,000 pills every day. The first and only chicken pharmacy in the world was featured in *National Geographic* and *Ripley's Believe It or Not*.

Petrolia

The first oil well in California was drilled in Petrolia.

Pismo Beach

Pismo Dunes State Vehicular Recreation Area is an outdoor enthusiast's delight.

Pismo Beach is the only beachside community on Highway 101 between Santa Barbara and San Francisco. It is also the only oceanfront community where automobiles may be driven on portions of the beach.

The greatest number of clams along the state's coastline are found in Pismo Beach and Pismo State Beach.

Placerville

As the flecks of gold were discovered along the banks of the American River, murders and robberies became commonplace. After one such crime in 1849 the jury clamored for a hanging. A giant oak was selected for what would become the first hanging in the Mother Lode country. The town of Placerville became known as Hangtown and by 1854 was the third largest town in California, surpassed only by San Francisco and Sacramento.

Hangtown's Gold Bug Park encompasses 61.5 acres and includes the only mine in California on public property. The mine has a dirt floor and no lighting, necessitating hard hats and flashlights to visit mining as it once was.

ROBERT HOLMES/CALTOUR

Pismo Dunes State Vehicular Recreation Area.

John Studebaker's work with a variety of carriage businesses in Placerville eventually progressed to the Studebaker automobile business.

Plumas County

The county contains the world's largest ponderosa pine tree. It is 227 feet tall, 24 feet around, and 7.5 feet in diameter. The tree is located near Bucks Lake in Plumas National Forest. The Harman Bar hiking trail leads to it.

Lassen Volcanic National Park, located in several counties including Plumas, has the world's largest plug dome volcano. It last erupted in 1914. Lassen Peak is the southernmost volcano in the Cascade Range, which extends from California into Canada.

The last transcontinental railroad line to be built in the United States was the Western Pacific line, completed in Plumus County in 1909. Western Pacific operated from 1910 to 1982, offering service from Oakland, California. After 1982 it merged and became part of Union Pacific.

Plumas Eureka Ski Bowl dates back to 1860. It is the site of the oldest recorded sport skiing and racing in the western hemisphere. Early day longboard ski racers descended a 2,600-foot run at speeds up to 90 miles per hour.

Fun facts

- California has three active volcanoes: In the Cascade Mountain range are Mt. Lassen (elevation 10,457 feet), a plug-dome volcano surrounded by volcanic hot springs, and Mount Shasta (elevation 14,162 feet), characterized by strong granite peaks; Mount Mammoth (elevation 11,000 feet) is found in the Sierra Nevada.

Point Reyes Station

Point Reyes Station has its faults. Point Reyes National Seashore's 0.6-mile Earthquake Trail runs along the San Andreas Fault Zone, one of California's most notorious fault lines. The trailhead is across the parking lot from the Bear Valley Visitor Center.

Pomona

Los Angeles County Fair is the largest county fair in the United States. (See Los Angeles County entry for further details.)

Pope Valley

Hubcaps and bottles can be found all around Hubcap Ranch. Designated as California Historical Landmark #939, the folk art environment is the creation of Emanuele "Litto" Damonte (1896–1985). His family continues to collect and display an array of hubcaps, now numbering more than 5,000.

Porterville

In the 1870s Porterville became the first Central Valley community to light its main street by electricity.

Portola

Railroad Days, held in August in Portola, is a celebration of California's important railroading heritage. Included during the weekend celebration is a hobo stew cook-off, train rides, and railroad exhibits.

Prunedale

There is a city law on the books not allowing the installation of two bathtubs in the same house.

Q

Quincy

Annually the city hosts the world's oldest championship cribbage tournament.

Butterfly Botanical Area contains *Darlingtonia Californica*, a rare carnivorous pitcher plant species that grows only in the region from southern Oregon to northern California, where the Cascade and Sierra mountain ranges meet.

Freight trains still run along the Union Pacific Railroad trestle spanning Chandler Creek. Completed in 1910, the line was intended to be the last transcontinental railroad in the United States.

R

Rancho Cordova

Eppie's Great Race, featuring running, biking, and paddling activities, is the world's oldest triathlon. The paddling competitions are the biggest in the country. International participants of all ages and abilities compete during the one-day event.

Rancho Mirage

Desert European Motor Cars continues its reputation as the highest volume Rolls Royce dealership in the United States.

Red Bluff

The William B. Ide Adobe State Historic Park contains an adobe memorial to the first president of the California Republic.

The Tehama County Fairgrounds hosts the largest three-day rodeo in the United States.

Redding

Shasta Dam, built with 6.5 million cubic yards of concrete weighing 15 million tons, has the second largest dam mass in the United States. It is 602 feet high and 3,450 feet long. Its 487-foot-tall spillway is the tallest in the world. When water goes over the spillway it creates the largest manmade waterfall in California.

Portions of the historic town of Kennett are located under Shasta Lake. During the building of Shasta Dam much of the town was demolished and the area flooded to fill the dam.

Due to its proximity to Shasta Lake, Redding is identified as the "Houseboat Capital of the World." Shasta Lake, with 30,000 surface acres and 370 miles of shoreline, is California's largest manmade lake.

California's first Masonic Lodge building, built in 1854, is still in use. The three-story building was originally built to house a mercantile business. When the business went bankrupt in 1859, the

Pit River Bridge.

Masonic Lodge acquired the entire building and Masons have been meeting there regularly ever since.

Pit River Bridge, spanning Shasta Lake, is the largest double-decker bridge in the world. Autos use the top deck and trains use the lower one.

Redlands

There is a city law on the books forbidding driving on city streets unless a man with a lantern walks ahead of the vehicle.

Redondo Beach

Each May the city of Redondo Beach hosts the largest outdoor wine-tasting celebration in southern California.

Richmond

Point Pinhole was the last site of the Giant Powder Company, the first company in America to produce dynamite.

Ridgecrest

The Burro Schmidt Tunnel measures 2,000 feet burrowed through solid rock. Burro Schmidt dug the tunnel by hand for nearly 40 years.

The Trona Pinnacles consist of more than 500 spires, some as high as 140 feet. They are the most outstanding example of tufa towers in North America. Formed during an early glacial period, the pinnacles represent the result of several geologic conditions causing carbonate towers to form.

Little Petroglyph Canyon holds the largest collection of ancient Indian rock art in North America.

Riverside

The city of Riverside is the home of the first navel orange tree in the nation. The annual Orange Blossom Festival, held in April, celebrates the city's relationship to the beginning of the citrus industry. During the event, Gourmet Grove features the area's finest chefs preparing orange-flavored food delicacies.

The first public showing of *Gone with the Wind* was held at the Fox Theater located in historic downtown Riverside.

Mount Roubidoux was the site of the first Easter sunrise service in California.

Rough & Ready

The small hamlet seceded from the Union in 1850 and did not legally return until 1948.

S

Sacramento

Sacramento was selected to be California's state capital in 1854. It boasts a gold-domed state capitol built in a Roman Corinthian style. Surrounding Capitol Park features native plants, gardens, and monuments.

The California State Railroad Museum is the largest museum of its kind in North America.

In 1853 the camellia flower was introduced to Sacramento from the East Coast. Today the camellia is the official flower of Sacramento as well as the namesake for the Camellia Festival held each year.

Samuel Clemens (a.k.a. Mark Twain) was a special news correspondent with the *Sacramento Union* newspaper in 1866.

Renovation of the state capitol in 1976 was the largest restoration project in United States history at that time.

Blue Diamond, the world's largest almond processing plant, is in Sacramento. On a busy day during harvest season more than 12 million pounds of almonds from around the world are delivered to the plant for processing.

Towe Ford Museum has the most comprehensive collection of antique Fords in the world.

James Marshall died a broken, penniless man thirty years after discovering gold near Sacramento and starting the California gold rush. Marshall asked the state for a $200 monthly pension "for recognition of this considerable service." He received the pension for one year, got half of it the next, and the pension was discontinued after that.

The transcontinental railroad started in Sacramento. It began with the initial meeting of its financial backers Leland Stanford,

ROBERT HOLMES/CALTOUR

Capitol Building in Sacramento.

Charles Crocker, Collis P. Huntington, and Mark Hopkins—also known as the "Big Four"—and the railroad designer Theodore Dehone Judah. This first meeting was held above a hardware store in November 1860.

Johann Breunar came to California to find gold but eventually got into making and selling furniture. In 1868 Breuner contracted to manufacture desks for the senate and assembly chambers of the state capitol. The desks he provided still serve the California legislators.

Tower Records was founded and still exists in Sacramento. Clayton Solomon and his son began the company in a drugstore, selling used jukebox records for 10 cents each.

In 1860, the Pony Express began a 1,980-mile-long mail delivery service between Sacramento and St. Joseph, Missouri. The company required 200 relay stations, 500 horses, and 80 riders to provide the ten-day service.

Crocker Art Museum is the oldest art museum west of the Mississippi.

Salinas

Born in Salinas, prolific writer John Steinbeck's influence is felt throughout the community. The National Steinbeck Center museum is dedicated to the life and works of the Nobel and Pulitzer Prize-winning author who penned such classic novels as *Cannery Row, Of Mice and Men, East of Eden, The Pearl,* and *The Grapes of Wrath.* The one-of-a-kind camper designed and used by Steinbeck during his journey "in search of America" recorded in *Travels with Charley* is a keystone display at the museum.

The Salinas Valley is known as the "Salad Bowl of the Nation" and grows more than 60 percent of the fresh vegetables consumed in the United States.

Salton Sea

Located more than 230 feet below sea level, the Salton Sea is California's largest lake. Summer temperatures in the area often reach the range of 120 degrees. The Salton Sea State Recreation Area's Salton Trough is the largest continental rift on the North American continent.

The world's fastest, longest, and saltiest personal watercraft race occurs on the Salton Sea. The event features 80 to 100 high-powered boats traveling a 15-mile course 20 times, for a total of 300 miles. The Salton Sea is known as the fastest lake on the continent because its high salt content and low elevation provide an efficient and buoyant surface for speedboats.

San Andreas

The notorious highwayman "Black Bart" was captured in San Francisco and sent to the county jail in San Andreas for trial. He

Fun facts

· The Monterey Sanctuary encompasses 5,312 square miles (4,024 nautical miles) from just north of the Golden Gate south past Big Sur to San Simeon, making it the largest marine sanctuary in the United States. The nation's eleventh designated national marine sanctuary extends along the northern California Coast.

was tried, convicted, and sentenced to spend 6 years in San Quentin State Prison. The original Calaveras County Courthouse & Jail still stands.

The first local newspaper was published on September 24, 1846.

California Caverns claims the distinction of being the most extensive system of caverns and passageways in the Mother Lode region.

San Bernardino County

Totaling nearly 3 million acres, San Bernardino County is the largest county in the country.

A program is underway involving the largest land acquisition in state history. The purpose is to protect the county and some land around it from further development and to protect sensitive habitats and potential recreation areas. The region being considered is composed of nearly 500,000 acres of California desert between Barstow and Needles and includes Mojave National Preserve and Joshua Tree National Park. Also included are critical habitats for the endangered desert tortoise, bighorn sheep, and the native bigelow cholla cactus

Silverwood Lake State Recreation Area includes the highest reservoir in the California State Water Project. It lies more than 3,300 feet above sea level.

At Kingston Range Wilderness, a small stand of white fir grows at the upper elevations of Kingston Peak. More than 500 plant species make this region one of the most botanically diverse within the California desert.

The Mohave Indians refer to the Piute Mountains as "Kwikantsoka" and consider them sacred.

Rodman Mountains Wilderness contains one of seven core raptor breeding areas. The area also provides habitat for rare prairie falcons and golden eagles.

Trilobite Wilderness is named for the fossils found within the region. The mountain range also is home to one of the larger and most rapidly growing desert bighorn sheep herds in the eastern Mojave Desert.

San Clemente

San Clemente was the first planned community in California. Envisioned by Ole Hanson, who called it "Spanish Village by the Sea" in 1925, the original design called for all buildings to be constructed with white stucco and red tile roofs. In 1932 the Ole Hanson Beach Club hosted the United States Olympic swimming trials.

SAN DIEGO CONVENTION & VISITORS BUREAU

Mission San Diego de Alcala.

President Richard Nixon chose a shoreline home in the town as the site of his "Western White House."

San Diego

San Diego Wild Animal Park has the largest collection of rhinoceroses in captivity. The first successful breeding of a pair of California condors in captivity took place at the park in 1988. The park hosts the largest chrysanthemum festival on the West Coast in late October and early November.

Star of India is the oldest active tall ship in the world. It is anchored at the San Diego Maritime Museum along with *The Berkeley,* the first successful propeller-driven ferryboat on the West Coast.

There is a city law on the books making it illegal to shoot jackrabbits from the back of a streetcar.

Mission San Diego de Alcala, founded in 1769, was the first in a chain of 21 missions that eventually stretched from San Diego to Sonoma. It all began when Father Serra, Father Palou, and Father Parron dug a hole 8 feet into the beachhead near the mouth of the San Diego River and planted a cross in it. Restoration of the mission began in 1931. The building retains its original facade and belfry base.

Fun facts

State Tree: The California Redwood

The tree, which is found in both the coastal and High Sierra regions, is among the most ancient of all living things. It exists in large, forested areas, predominantly in California.

Torrey Pines State Reserve and State Beach was established to help protect one of two remaining torrey pine forests in the world and also a rare botanical dinosaur. The other remaining torrey pine forest is on Santa Rosa Island and is part of Channel Islands National Park.

Cabrillo Bridge, built prior to the 1915 Panama-California Exposition as an entrance to Balboa Park, was the first multiple-arched, cantilever-type bridge built in California. Secretary of the Navy Franklin D. Roosevelt was the first person to drive across it.

The Old Globe Theatre, located in Balboa Park, is California's oldest professional theater.

In 1927 pilot Charles Lindberg made his first flight ever in the *Spirit of St. Louis*, from a San Diego airfield along Barnett Avenue. About one month later he took to the skies again for his historic, 33.5-hour transatlantic flight from New York to Paris.

J. J., an orphaned California gray whale brought to SeaWorld in January 1997, was the largest animal any zoological facility in the world had ever attempted to rehabilitate. J. J. was also the first

ROBERT HOLMES/CALTOUR

Cabrillo National Monument.

and only California gray whale ever to be rescued, rehabilitated, and returned to the sea. After her rehabilitation, she was released into the Pacific Ocean.

The San Diego Zoo features the only nudist colony exhibit in a zoo: the naked mole rats in the children's section. The zoo is also home to the nation's largest Galapagos tortoise colony. The first open heart surgery performed at the zoo was on Karen, an orangutan.

The world's largest outdoor pipe organ, the Spreckels Organ, brightens Balboa Park with musical sounds.

Mount Palomar Observatory's Hale telescope was the world's largest working single-lens telescope when it was installed in 1947.

San Diego is considered California's oldest city. The Cabrillo National Monument on Point Loma peninsula, memorializing Juan Rodriguez Cabrillo's arrival in the area on September 28, 1542, is second only to the Statue of Liberty as the most visited national monument in the United States.

Mission Trail Regional Park is the largest urban park in California. It has more than 5,800 acres to explore.

The Point Loma Lighthouse dominates the Point Loma Preserve. It was one of the first Pacific Coast lighthouses.

San Fernando Valley

The world's longest mural, *Great Wall of Los Angeles*, stretches nearly 2,500 feet along the Los Angeles River. Created by young artists, it depicts immigrants in Los Angeles.

San Francisco

San Francisco has the most wooden Victorian homes of any city in the world—approximately 14,000.

San Francisco was home to the first California State Fair in 1854.

The legendary Westin St. Francis hotel and the lounge, The Compass Rose, witnessed the birth of the martini in the 1940s.

Known as the crookedest street in the world, residential Lombard Street has nine hairpin curves and switchbacks to challenge drivers. But Lombard Street is not the only crooked street in San Francisco. Some people claim that unassuming Vermont Street, tucked behind a highway entrance ramp in the Potrero Hill neighborhood, has even more switchbacks.

The steepest San Francisco roadways are Filbert, between Leavenworth and Hyde, and 22nd Street, between Church and Vicksburg. The longest street is Mission (7.29 miles); the widest is Sloat Boulevard (135 feet); and the narrowest is DeForest Way (4.5 feet).

SAN FRANCISCO CONVENTION & VISITORS BUREAU

San Francisco Cable Car.

Golden Gate National Recreation Area is the most popular recreation area in the United States national park system. It includes 114 square miles of open space, 110 miles of trails, 78 shipwrecks, 23 rare and endangered species, 1,200 historic structures, 12 sandy beaches, 100 historic forts, 5 lighthouses, 2 redwood forests, and the Golden Gate Bridge.

Since the Golden Gate Bridge opened in 1937, more than 1,200 people have died after plunging 220 feet from the famous span.

The Transamerica Pyramid is the city's tallest building at 853 feet. Mission Dolores, dedicated on August 2, 1791, is the oldest building in the city.

Founded in 1962, the Judah L. Magnes Museum was the first Jewish museum ever accredited by the American Association of Museums. It houses the third largest collection of Jewish ceremonial and folk art in the United States.

Fourteen islands lie in San Francisco Bay—12 are within San Francisco city limits. Alcatraz Island was once the site of the toughest maximum security prison in the United States. Other islands include the Farallones, a group of seven islands; Treasure Island; Yerba Buena; Angel Island; and Red Rock.

Immigration Station on Angel Island opened in 1910 and closed during World War I to stem the tide of immigrants.

Chinatown is located along Grant Avenue, the city's oldest street. It is where Johnny Kan opened the first authentic Chinese restaurant in America in 1939. The first Chinese-style building on Washington Street is also the site where California's first newspaper was printed.

The famous San Francisco cable cars had their inaugural run on August 2, 1873. On October 1, 1964, they were declared a National

Historic Landmark—the only moving landmark in the United States.

There are 43 hills within the city's boundary. Major ones are Twin Peaks (910 feet and 903 feet), Nob (376 feet), Russian (294 feet), and Telegraph (248 feet).

The Pacific Telephone building on New Montgomery Street has the honor of being the first skyscraper built in San Francisco. It houses the Telephone Pioneer Communications Museum.

The city's oldest restaurant, Tadich Grill, opened in 1849.

Domingo Ghirardelli arrived in the United States in 1849 and became a purveyor of chocolate and other products to gold rush pioneers.

The city's first coffee-roasting plant opened in 1850 and later became J. A. Folger & Company of Folgers coffee fame.

Fior d'Italia is the oldest Italian restaurant in the United States.

Chicken tetrazzini was invented in San Francisco in 1908 for Luisa Tetrazzini, an Italian coloratura.

Celery Victor was invented in 1910 at the St. Francis Hotel.

Crab Louis was invented in 1914 at Solari's Restaurant.

Green Goddess salad dressing was invented in 1915 at the Palace Hotel at the request of actor George Arlis while he was starring in the play *Green Goddess.*

In 1939 the first authentic Chinese food delivery service in the United States opened at the Chinese Kitchen.

"Trader Vic" Bergeron invented the Mai Tai cocktail in San Francisco in 1944.

Irish Coffee was developed at the Buena Vista Cafe in 1952.

The first ship-to-shore message in the United States was transmitted in 1899 when a lightship near the Golden Gate sent a dot-and-dash message to a receiving unit onshore announcing the return of the first troops from the Spanish-American War.

The annual California International Antiquarian Book Fair is billed as the world's largest rare book fair in the world. It is sanctioned by the Antiquarian Booksellers Association of America. Selection includes early printed books and manuscripts, illustrated books, fine bindings, early American literature, and much more. It is held alternately in Los Angeles and San Francisco.

In 1945, the city hosted delegates from around the world who came to the United States to draw up the charter for the United Nations.

San Gorgonio

The 56,749-acre San Gorgonio Wilderness runs along the summit of the San Bernardino mountain range, the highest range in southern California. Within the wilderness are meadows, lakes, and two major trails.

San Jose

San Jose, the first civil settlement in California, was established in 1777. In 1849 the community became the site of the first California state capitol.

Peralta Adobe, built in 1797, is the city's oldest existing structure. San Jose's first federal building, built in 1892, now houses the San Jose Museum of Art.. In 1857, San Jose State University became California's first institution of higher learning. Most prominent among the campus's landmarks is an ivy covered tower built in 1910.

Dr. Charles Herrold established the first regularly transmitting radio station in the world in 1909. The station was located in San Jose. Because Herrold operated without a license, a Pennsylvania station, KDKA, is often credited as the first radio station licensed to broadcast.

In 1884, Sarah Winchester began a construction project that occupied carpenters and craftsmen until her death thirty-eight years later. The Winchester Mystery House holds the Guinness world record for being the home under continuous construction for the longest amount of time.

San Juan Bautista

Founded in 1797, San Juan Bautista Mission was unwittingly built directly above the San Andreas earthquake fault. Much of the original structure remains and has been restored to once again be the largest California mission church and the only one with three aisles.

San Juan Capistrano

Swallows return to San Juan Capistrano Mission every year to build their nests. Legend says that the swallows return to their nesting places on the walls and arches of the mission on March 19 each year, but their arrival can actually pre- and postdate that specific day. It is also said that many years more pigeons than swallows visit the mission. The return of the swallows was first recorded by missionaries in the late 1700s. (Evidence suggests that the birds nested in siltstone cliffs near the ocean long before the mission was built.) The first published account of the swallows appeared in 1930 in a book called *Capistrano Nights*. In it, Acu, an old mission bell ringer, tells Father St. John O'Sullivan the legend of the swallows.

A gilded altarpiece illuminates the Serra Chapel of 1777, the oldest building still in use in California and the only surviving church where Father Serra, the founder of the 21 California missions, said Mass.

The bell tower of the New Parish Church is the tallest structure in town.

San Luis Obispo

San Luis Obispo is home to one of the most curious perpetual folk art projects in the world. And the public is invited to participate. Bubble Gum Alley is a walkway between old brick walls adorned with thousands of wads of bubble gum in various colors and shapes. The alley has been featured in numerous magazines, television programs, and books.

San Luis Obispo de Tolosa was the first mission to use tiles extensively on the roof. Tiles were used after repeated attacks by Indians who used flaming arrows to ignite the original thatched roof.

San Marino

The Huntington Library, Art Collection, and Botanical Gardens provide one of California's premier attractions. The Huntington Library's grounds are a popular and sought after filming location. The estate is seen in the feature films *Coming to America, MacArthur,* and *War and Remembrance.* The Huntington Botanical

Fun facts

- California has more than 420 recreational lakes.

Gardens offers 15 separate gardens and includes the largest collection of cacti and succulents in North America. The Huntington's Palm and Jungle Garden houses the largest collection of palm trees on the West Coast.

Los Robles estate was the site of San Marino's first community Christmas tree, San Gabriel Valley's first schoolhouse, and the state's first tennis club.

San Mateo County

Crystal Springs Dam is the world's largest concrete dam.

San Miguel

San Miguel Arcangel (San Miguel Mission) was founded in 1797. A self-guided tour includes the crucifix from the original main altar, artifacts from the mission's early days, an old beehive oven, a Spanish strong box, and a cemetery where more than 2,000 Native Americans are buried.

San Pedro

The only remaining wooden lighthouse in California is on the edge of a cliff in Point Fermin Park. The lighthouse was built in 1874 on a promontory that gave it the most commanding view of the ocean on the southern California coast. It functioned as a lighthouse until 1942. It is now the residence of the park superintendent.

San Rafael

China Camp State Park preserves one of the earliest and largest of the Chinese fishing villages that once thrived in the region.

George Lucas used the city of San Rafael to create the quintessential small town in *American Graffiti*.

San Simeon

Hearst Castle is the largest California estate to come into public hands with its original collections intact. William Randolph Hearst inherited the land and with famed San Francisco architect Julia Morgan collaborated to build one of the world's greatest showplaces. The estate has 165 rooms and 127 acres of gardens, pools, and walkways. The facility exhibits the largest collection of European antiquities in the California state parks system.

San Ysidro

The world's busiest international border crossing—with more than 60 million crossings each year—is located in San Ysidro.

Sanger

Wonder Valley celebrates being both California's first dude ranch and the legendary hideout of the notorious Dalton gang.

Since the 1920s the city has featured a holiday trek to what's been dubbed locally as the "Nation's Christmas Tree." The celebration begins in Sanger on the second Sunday in December. The 267-foot-tall giant sequoia is one of the oldest living things on earth. The tree, known as the General Grant Tree, was approximately 2,000 years old when Christ was born.

Santa Barbara

Mission Santa Barbara is the only mission church ever built with two towers.

The Moreton Bay Fig towers as the nation's largest tree of its kind. It has a span of more than 160 feet and provides more than 21,000 square feet of shade.

Due to its extensive fish population, Cachuma Lake is considered the best place in southern California to see bald eagles in their natural habitat. The American bald eagle is one of the largest raptors in California. Its talons enable it to catch fish swimming close to the surface of the water. In the winter the eagles migrate to the lake from as far away as Alaska in search of a warmer climate and an abundant food supply.

El Presidio de Santa Barbara State Historic Park contains the oldest structure in the California state parks system—the Canedo Adobe, built in 1782. El Cuartel, built in 1788, is the only building of the Santa Barbara Presidio remaining intact.

Santa Catalina Island

Avalon is the only city on Santa Catalina Island.

In a state known for its dependence on the automobile, the village of Avalon on Santa Catalina Island restricts the number of automobiles allowed in town by issuing limited auto permits. Residents and visitors rely on walking, bicycles, or electric carts. Avalon was the first city in California empowered by the state legislature to control the number, size, speed, and noise of vehicles operating within the city limits.

Founded in 1889, the Tuna Club serves as the oldest fishing club in the United States. It attracted the likes of Cecil B. DeMille, John Wayne, Bing Crosby, Charlie Chaplin, Theodore Roosevelt, Zane Grey, and Winston Churchill to its rich sport fishing waters.

The Casino Building, Catalina's world-famous landmark, boasts a circular ballroom upstairs that has the largest dance floor of its kind in existence today. In the 1930s and 1940s the ballroom hosted many of the big bands including Jimmy Dorsey, Woody Herman, and Harry James.

The island's wilderness interior is home to thousands of species of native plants and animals, many of which are found nowhere else in the world. The Catalina Island Fox and the Beechey Ground Squirrel exist only on Santa Catalina.

The Avalon Theatre was the first theater designed for sound movies prior to its actual construction.

In 1926 American author Zane Grey built a pueblo-style home on the hillside overlooking Avalon Bay. He spent most of his later life in Avalon writing and fishing. The home is now a hotel and includes many of Grey's original furnishings.

The waters of Avalon are home to the only two semi-submersible vessels in the United States.

The world's first wireless telegraph station was built on Santa Catalina in 1902.

Pigeons were used to carry messages between Santa Catalina and the mainland from the 1850s to as late as 1899.

The Catalina Island Golf Course, built in 1892, was the first golf course in southern California.

Santa Clara

Mission Santa Clara was the first California mission to honor a woman—Clare of Assisi. It once had the largest Native American population of all the California missions.

Santa Clara University is the oldest institution of higher learning in the state.

NASA/AMES Research Center includes the largest wind tunnel, research aircraft, and flight operation facilities in the world.

Paramount's Great America's hometown is Santa Clara.

Approximately 90,000 bags of cotton candy are sold each season to guests. That is about five bags per day, every day for 48 years, for each person visiting the park each season.

Columbia Carousel has been recognized as the world's tallest double-decker carousel.

The pinnacle on Carousel Columbia was used as an ornate potbellied stove in the movie *Marie Antoinette*. The caps on the 121 supporting columns came from *The Swan*, a movie starring Grace Kelly.

The design for Greased Lightnin', the park's shuttle loop coaster, was based on catapults developed by the Germans to launch V2 rockets during World War II.

Sky Tower is the tallest observation structure in northern California.

Actor Fess Parker owned the land on which Paramount's Great America was built. The land was being used to farm zucchini.

Among the celebrities on hand for the park's opening were Clint Eastwood, Merv Griffin, Lynda Day George, Roy Rogers, and Dale Evans.

Project Stealth roller coaster is the world's first true flying coaster. Guests ride up the lift hill backward, are reclined so they are parallel with the track, then are inverted during the first drop. They spend the rest of the ride flying on their stomachs and backs.

Santa Cruz

Año Nuevo State Reserve houses and protects elephant seals, the northern hemisphere's largest members of the seal and sea lion family. The reserve is located approximately 20 miles north of Santa Cruz.

The coastal city is home to the O'Neil Company, inventor of the wetsuit and manufacturer of surfboards.

Frazier Lewis invented the first candy bar, named a Victoria Cream, in Santa Cruz. The recipe was later sold to movie star ZaSu Pitts, an avid candymaker who grew up in the town.

Big Basin Redwoods State Park is the oldest California state park. The Joss House, located in the park, was built in 1874 on the site of an earlier temple.

Lighthouse Point contains the world's first surfing museum. It is located in the hull of a lighthouse at Steamer Lane, Santa Clara County's most famous surfing spot.

Kathryn Sullivan, a graduate of the University of California Santa Cruz, became the first American woman to walk in space.

Santa Cruz Beach Boardwalk's hometown is Santa Cruz.

A California Historical Landmark, the Boardwalk bills itself as the only major seaside amusement park remaining on the entire West Coast.

ROBERT HOLMES/CALTOUR

Santa Cruz Beach Boardwalk.

The park's oldest rides—the 1911 Looff Carousel and the 1924 Giant Dipper roller coaster—are both National Historic Landmarks. The Giant Dipper roller coaster is California's oldest coaster; it is among the oldest operating coasters in the country.

The 1911 Looff Carousel, which still runs in its original location, has a working catch-the-ring machine, one of only a handful left in the nation.

Marini's Salt Water Taffy is still made with the original 1924 taffy-pulling machine and a wrapping machine that is just as old. The first Marini concessionaire at the Boardwalk started in 1915 and stores are still run by family members.

Santa Cruz Beach Boardwalk plays a starring roll in hundreds of television shows, commercials, and movies. Two of the best-known films include Clint Eastwood's *Sudden Impact* and the 1987 comic-horror hit *The Lost Boys*.

Santa Cruz County

In 1769 the men of the Portola Expedition became the first non-natives to traverse the county's coastline.

Salz Tannery is the oldest tannery in California. It is the last survivor of what was once a major industry in the county.

Santa Maria

The "Barbecue Capital of the World" is famous for its tri-tip barbecue and for streetside grilling by local restaurants and nonprofit organizations.

The community was first known as Central City, but the name was changed when the Pacific Coast Railroad arrived, because often mail intended for Central City, California, ended up in Central City, Colorado.

Santa Monica

Pacific Park, on the venerable Santa Monica Pier, re-creates the amusement parks that could once be found all along the Pacific Coast. Included among the rides is the 1910-vintage hand-carved merry-go-round that appeared in the movie *The Sting*.

The Santa Monica airport is the busiest one-runway facility in the nation.

There is a city law on the books forbidding the playing of a percussion instrument on the beach.

Former child star Shirley Temple was born in Santa Monica. During her childhood, her famous curls always numbered 56. The curls were part of her charm and were set by her mother, who always made sure the number was exactly the same.

Santa Paula

Union Oil Company (now Unocal) began in 1890. The brick structure where the business originated is now the California Oil Museum. It is considered the finest oil museum in the state. One display features the worst flood in the United States in terms of lives lost. The flooding occurred when the St. Francis Dam above Santa Paula burst in 1928.

Santa Rosa

Horticulturist Luther Burbank made his home in Santa Rosa for more than 50 years. The Luther Burbank Home & Gardens showcases more than 600 varieties of plants, fruits, and vegetables he created.

Robert Ripley, promoter of the curious and extraordinary, was born in the community on Christmas Day, 1893. He became a world-famous cartoonist with his daily "Believe It or Not" feature, read by millions of people throughout the world. Ripley is buried in Santa Rosa Memorial Park. His efforts continue in newspapers worldwide and serve as the basis for "Ripley's Believe It or Not" attractions.

Charles Schulz produced his famed "Peanuts" comic strip in Santa Rosa. Schulz was the most widely syndicated cartoonist in history and had his work published in more than 2,300 newspapers.

Scotia

Scotia is one of the few company towns left in the United States. It was built by the Pacific Lumber Company, which operates the world's largest redwood lumber mill in Scotia.

Selma

Known as the "Raisin Capital of the World," the small city produces approximately 95 percent of the raisins sold in the United States. The annual Selma Raisin Festival is held in May.

Shasta County

Fall River Valley produces 25 percent of the wild rice marketed in the world.

Shoshone

The desert area around Shoshone straddles the border between California and Nevada. Owned entirely by Susan Sorrels, the town consists of a few buildings along Highway 127 heading into Death Valley. Early miners carved dwellings in nearby sandstone cliffs, thus constructing homes that were cool in the hot summer environment. The historic residences include windows, walls of sandstone, dirt floors, and occasional shelves carved into the walls.

Sierra Madre

The giant Chinese Wisteria planted in Sierra Madre is the largest blossoming plant on earth. It has branches 500 feet long, covers nearly an acre, weighs 252 tons, and has an estimated 1.5 million blossoms during its blossoming period of five weeks.

Simi Valley

The only United States president to have had an acting career is honored at the Ronald Reagan Presidential Library & Museum located on a hilltop overlooking the Simi Valley. The state-of-the-art museum displays take visitors from Reagan's early years to his life as a world leader. The facility is one of two educational and entertaining presidential structures in California.

Siskiyou County

Mount Shasta, rising 14,162 feet above sea level, is recognized as the tallest volcano in California and the second tallest in the United States.

Until the end of the twentieth century, Humbolt martens were thought to be extinct. Then the animals were discovered in the remote Siskiyou Wilderness.

Captain Jack's Stronghold, located in what is now Lava Beds National Monument, was the site of the climactic battle of the Modoc War of 1872–75. It is thought to be the only major Indian battle fought in California.

Klamath Basin National Wildlife Refuge has the largest winter population of bald eagles in the continental United States.

The last horse-drawn stagecoach robbery occurred on July 5, 1908, on the old stage road from Yreka to Fort Jones.

The largest gold exhibit south of Alaska, valued at over $1 million, may be viewed at the Siskiyou County Courthouse, located in Yreka.

Smith River

Smith River bills itself as the "Easter Lily Capital of the World." Area growing facilities produce thousands of Easter lily plants each year.

Solano County

Mare Island Naval Shipyard, the West Coast's first naval installation, was established in 1854.

Soledad

Nuestra Señora de la Soledad (Soledad Mission) is the burial site of Jose Joaquin de Arrellaga, who served as governor of California from 1792–94 and 1804–14. The mission's original bell, cast in Mexico in 1799, still hangs outside the chapel.

Solvang

Founded by Danish educators in 1911, Solvang is known as the "Danish Capital of America."

Sonoma

The original San Francisco Solano mission was mostly washed away by a tremendous thunderstorm. Today Sebastian Vineyards includes much of the mission's original vineyard.

The first recorded expedition into Napa County occurred when Franciscan Padre Jose Altamira scouted sites for the northernmost California mission. Mission San Francisco Solano de Sonoma was built in 1823 and was the last to be built of California's 21 missions. Each year the "Blessing of the Grapes" is performed in front of the mission by a Franciscan priest.

The annual Vintage Festival is the oldest wine festival in the state.

The first raising of California's bear flag took place in Sonoma in 1846. Less than two months later the area became a territory of the United States. Bear Flag Monument now stands where California declared itself a republic, flew the bear flag, and a few days later replaced it with the Stars and Stripes.

There is a city law on the books prohibiting wiping one's car down with used underwear.

The ancient redwood forest within Armstrong Redwoods State Reserve contains the largest remaining old-growth redwood forest in Sonoma County. The coast redwoods are among the world's tallest and oldest living things.

Sonora

At 355 feet long, Knights Ferry is the longest covered bridge in California and the longest authentic covered bridge west of the Mississippi. The bridge was built in 1864 and is part of the Knights Ferry Recreation Area on the Stanislaus River.

Stinson Beach

One of the coast's most popular nude beaches is located a mile south of downtown Stinson Beach.

Fun facts

State Song: "I Love You, California"

"I Love You, California" was written by F. B. Silverwood. It was designated the state song in 1951 and became the official state song in 1988.

Surprise Valley

The Bureau of Land Management developed a loop tour along the Surprise Valley/Barrel Springs backcountry byways. The tour offers evidence of giant earthquakes and volcanoes, a prehistoric lake, remnants of fossils and prehistoric art, and the final resting places of Calvary troopers.

T

Taft

The Kern Oil Museum keeps alive the memory of California's oil industry by displaying a 1917 wooden oil derrick at its original site.

Tarzana

The city was named for Tarzan, the central character in the Edgar Rice Burroughs' series of popular novels which began with *Tarzan of the Apes* in 1914. Born in Chicago, Burroughs lived in what is now the city of Tarzana. He died in the California community of Encino.

Robert Holmes/CalTour

Tehachapi Scenic Wind Farm.

Tehachapi

Recognized as one of the greatest engineering feats in railroading, the Tehachapi Loop, designed in the 1870s, allows trains to gain 2,735 feet in elevation in just 16 miles. Freight trains use the loop to climb the mountain between California's central valley and the Mojave Desert, circling around and over themselves as they move up the mountain.

A Tehachapi Scenic Wind Farm tour travels through 5,000 wind turbines located in Tehachapi Pass. More than half a dozen companies operate turbines in the area, producing enough power to meet the needs of 250,000 homes. Each year the Tehachapi Wind Fair celebrates the region's natural resources.

Temecula

Temecula Valley International Film Festival has the distinction of being the only film festival in the world to feature exclusively romantic comedies in the full-length categories.

In the early 1920s and 1930s, prize fighters Jack Dempsey and Jack Sharkey worked out in a makeshift ring on the second floor of the old Welty Building at the intersection of Front Street and Main Street over the Blind Pig Saloon.

There is a city law on the books giving ducks the right of way to cross Rancho California Street, no matter what.

Butterfield Overland Stagecoach Company and California's first inland post office were established in the area now known as the city's "Old Town."

Three Rivers

Sequoia and Kings Canyon National Parks contain the largest cave system in California. Giant Forest contains groups of giant sequoias and is home to the General Sherman Tree, the world's largest living thing. The tree weighs approximately 2.7 million pounds, has a height of 274.9 feet, a circumference of 102.6 feet, and grows enough new wood per year to make another 60-foot-tall tree.

Kings River Canyon, where Boyden Cavern is located, is the deepest canyon in the United States at 8,000 feet deep. It is located in Kings Canyon National Park.

Keweah Post Office contains one small room and a porch. It is one of the smallest post offices in operation in the United States.

Thousand Oaks

California Lutheran University's Scandinavian Festival is the largest, longest running gathering of Scandinavians in California.

Trona

Pinnacles National Natural Landmark, south of the community, features unique tufa towers. Some reach a height of 140 feet. Tufa is the result of calcium carbonate forming over the ground and building up into limestone mounds.

Truckee

It was November 1844 when the first wheeled vehicles crossed the Sierra Nevada. Men, women, and children pioneered the early emigrant route across the mountains into California. A Paiute named Truckee served these adventurers as a trail guide.

The Pioneer Monument in Donner Memorial State Park is a tribute to all pioneers who traveled the Truckee Route of the California Trail.

The 17-ton Rocking Stone seen on the downtown Truckee historical walking tour is 1 of 25 known rocking stones in the world. Native Americans used the rock for drying their food and for holding ceremonies. The stone has been shored up and no longer rocks.

Trinidad

Founded April 8, 1850, the town of Trinidad is considered the oldest town on the northern California coast.

Trinity County

Trinity Alps Wilderness covers 500,000 acres, making it the second largest wilderness area in California.

Trinity Lake, with 16,000 surface acres and 147 miles of shoreline, is the third largest lake in California.

ROBERT HOLMES/CALTOUR

Pioneer Monument.

Tulare County

Known as the "Milk Capital of the World," the county represents the second largest agricultural producing area in the United States and the number one milk producer in the world.

California Farm Equipment Show & International Exposition boasts being the largest farm equipment show in the world. The annual event features more than 1,000 exhibitors displaying the latest farm equipment and offering just about anything in the world to do with farming. The event is held at the International Agri-Center.

Tulelake

The "Horseradish Growing Capital of the World" grows more than one-third of the world's radish crop.

Medicine Lake Highlands is the largest identified volcano (in total area) within California. Driving is permitted on some slopes and into the caldera of the massive volcano.

Lava Beds National Monument's hometown is Tulelake.

> The national monument includes the highest concentration of lava tube caves in the world, the highest concentration of pictographs and petroglyphs in California, the longest lava tube cave in California (Mammoth Cave), the deepest lava tube cave in California (Crystal Cave), the largest obsidian flow in California and perhaps the world, and the highest concentration of bald eagles in the contiguous United States.
>
> The only major Indian war fought on California soil occurred at this location.

Tustin

Two blimp hangars, one in Tustin and another at the former Marine base at El Toro, were built to house dirigibles, also called blimps. The hangars are the largest wooden structures in the world.

Twentynine Palms

The largest Marine Corps base in the United States is located at Twentynine Palms.

U

Ukiah

Vichy Hot Springs Resort & Inn claims the only naturally warm and naturally carbonated mineral baths in North America.

Long recognized as helpful in stress reduction, the continuously operating mineral springs of Ukiah's Vichy Hot Springs Resort were discovered in the 1850s. Famous guests have included Mark Twain, Robert Louis Stevenson, Jack London, presidents Ulysses S. Grant, Benjamin Harrison, and Teddy Roosevelt, and pugilists John L. Sullivan and "Gentleman" Jim Corbett. More recent guests have included Wavy Gravy, Patch Adams, congressmen, senators, famous writers, and filmmakers.

A giant redwood tree located approximately 122 miles west of Ukiah has been identified as the world's tallest living thing. Standing at an awe-inspiring 367.5 feet, "Mendocino Tree" took the tallest designation from the previous record holder in California's Del Norte County. That tree once stood at 367.8 feet but lost 10 feet during a storm.

In front of an office building in town, a bronze plaque on a granite boulder reads "To the ladies of the night who plied their trade upon this site." The plaque is located about one block south of the courthouse.

Union City

In 1918 William Dreyer and Joseph Edy started Dreyer's and Edy's Grand Ice Cream. One year later they developed the world's first batch of Rocky Road ice cream and became a first-class maker of frozen yogurt and other frozen delicacies.

V

Valencia

Six Flags Magic Mountain's hometown is Valencia.

Magic Mountain's first roller coaster, Gold Rusher, opened in 1971.

Revolution opened with 3,457 feet of spiraling track. The coaster contains the nation's first 360-degree vertical loop.

Colossus features the world's largest dual-track wooden roller coaster.

Roaring Rapids is America's first whitewater rafting ride.

Free Fall is the first descending thrill-ride of its kind.

Ninja is the fastest suspended coaster on the West Coast featuring trains that swing freely from side to side.

The world's largest looping steel roller coaster, Viper, opened with cameras mounted on the track. This started the trend of photographing people as they ride.

Psyclone is a replica of New York's legendary Coney Island wooden coaster Cyclone.

Batman the Ride features two corkscrews and two vertical loops. The coaster is the centerpiece of the Gotham City Backlot.

Superman the Escape, reaching 100 miles per hour, is the world's fastest thrill-ride. At 415 feet, it's the tallest thrill-ride in the park.

Riddler's Revenge opened as the world's tallest and fastest stand-up roller coaster.

Bugs Bunny World is designed specifically to encourage adults and children to experience and ride its attractions together.

Goliath, one the first coasters to open in the year 2000, features a 255-foot drop into a 120-foot-long tunnel of darkness. The giant coaster travels at a speed of 85 miles per hour.

Vallecito

Moaning Cavern is the largest single-chamber public cavern in the state. The main room is large enough to fit the Statue of Liberty inside. Some of the cavern's formations reach 25 feet in height.

Vallejo

St. Peter's Chapel houses the oldest naval chapel in the United States and the largest collection of Tiffany stained-glass windows in the West.

Vallejo's Mare Island provided the first permanent dry dock on the West Coast. Construction on the historic granite dock was begun in 1878 and finished in 1901.

Six Flags Marine World's hometown is Vallejo.

The theme park is America's only combination wildlife park, oceanarium, and theme park.

Medusa is the fastest, tallest, and most technologically advanced roller coaster in northern California and the first floorless super-coaster on the West Coast.

The park's butterfly habitat is the first major walk-through facility of its kind in the western United States.

Van Nuys

The Van Nuys airport is the busiest two-runway airport in the nation.

Ventura

San Buenaventura Mission stands as the final mission founded by Father Junipero Serra. The mission is the only one in the United States once featuring bells made of wood. The mission displays the wooden bells in the onsite museum.

Channel Islands National Park is the only national park in southern California.

The world's first oil tanker burned and sank at the end of the Ventura Pier in 1887.

Ventura County

Located north of Ventura near the community of Ojai is 2,700-acre Lake Casitas, the biggest recreation lake in the county.

Visalia

Founded and named in 1852, the city is recognized as the oldest city between Los Angeles and Stockton.

The well-known "End of the Trail" statue was originally constructed of plaster of paris, two-by-fours, and chicken wire for the 1915 Panama Pacific International Exposition in San Francisco. The statue portrays the ultimate defeat of the American Indian and the closing of the western frontier. The large statue won the gold medal for statuary at the Exposition and at one time was the most copied artwork in the world. After being consigned to a scrap heap, the original statue was acquired by civic-minded Visalia citizens. It was later sold to the National Cowboy Hall of Fame in Oklahoma City but not before a bronze replica was made in exchange for the original. Since 1919 the replica has stood in Mooney Grove Park.

Volcano

The largest collection of grinding rock mortars in the world are found at Indian Grinding Rock State Park. Located along a walking trail, the 1,185 mortar rocks were once used for a variety of grinding needs espceially for acorns from the native oak trees. Called *chaw'se* by the Miwoks, each Indian woman reportedly had her own rock.

More than 400,000 volunteer-planted bulbs burst into spring each year at Daffodil Hill near Volcano. The planting began in 1877 and continues today.

CALIFORNIA STATE PARKS

Indian Grinding Rock State Park.

Walnut Creek

Mount Diablo State Park can be entered through Walnut Creek or Danville.

Mount Diablo State Park's summit is 3,849 feet above sea level and offers a sweeping panorama. More of the earth's surface can be seen from the mountain than any other peak in the world, except Mount Kilimanjaro in Africa.

Wasco

The "Rose Capital of the Nation" each year produces approximately 75 percent of all roses grown in the United States. The bushes mature in fields surrounding the community. An annual Festival of Roses is held in the city. The Wasco Rose Garden contains more than 1,000 rose bushes.

Watts

The Simon Rodia Towers in Watts make up the largest piece of folk art ever created by a single person. Popularly known as the Watts Towers, the three towers are the creation of Simon Rodia, a tile setter who labored on the project between 1921 and 1954. His remarkable folk art consists of concrete structures, shells, tile, pottery, and glass. The tallest of the towers is 104 feet high. The Simon Rodia State Historic Park is the state's smallest historic park at a mere 0.11 acre.

Weaverville

The Joss House, rebuilt in 1874, is acknowledged as California's oldest continuously used Chinese Temple.

Weaverville Drugstore, built in 1854, is characterized as the oldest continuously operated pharmacy in the West.

West Hollywood

Sunset Tower was the first all-electric apartment building in California.

Westwood

The town is the former home of the Red River Lumber Company, which operated the largest pine lumber mill in the world from 1913 to 1956.

Whiskeytown

Whiskeytown Shasta-Trinity National Recreation Area is the only place where *Puccinelli Howelli* (Howel's salt grass) grows.

President John F. Kennedy dedicated Whiskeytown Dam on September 28, 1962. A memorial, including an audio recording of the dedication speech, stands near the site of the dedication ceremony.

Willow Creek

Six Rivers National Forest is home to the world's largest Tanoak tree. It was placed on the National Register of Big Trees in 1991. It is 92 feet tall with a girth of 22.5 feet.

The legend and lore of Bigfoot abounds in the town. The story began with Native Americans who believed the manlike creature lived in the Bluff Creek area along the Klamath River The earliest reported Bigfoot sighting was in 1886. The town has a large Bigfoot statue, an annual Bigfoot Celebration, the Bigfoot Museum, and a map showing the many places it has been seen in the area.

Wilmington

The Drum Barracks was a military headquarters and remains a California Civil War landmark.

Woodlake

The biggest ranch rodeo in California is held at the Jackson Ranch, considered to be the most beautiful rodeo grounds in the United States.

Y

Yorba Linda

Richard Nixon, thirty-seventh president of the United States, was born in his parents' home in Yorba Linda in 1913. The residence of the president's birth has been restored and is the location of the Richard M. Nixon Library and Birthplace. The facility is one of two educational and entertaining presidential structures in California.

Yosemite

Shadow of the Giants Trail, located within the Nelder Grover Giant Sequoia Preservation Area, is an easy, 1-mile hike featuring giant California sequoia trees. The nearby 0.25-mile Cedars Interpretive Trail is designed especially to allow people with disabilities to experience the park's flora and fauna.

Yucaipa

The Yucaipa Adobe is thought to be the oldest house in San Bernardino County. The building showcases farming equipment and antiques from the early 1850s when the building was constructed.

Z

Zenia

Located in the remote southwestern corner of Trinity County, the tiny hamlet of Zenia is one of the state's most out-of-the way locations and has no accommodations. A country store down the road in nearby Kettenpom has gas and groceries.

Guided pig hunting is offered by local landowners.

Related Resources

A wealth of information is in print for individuals seeking information regarding California, the Golden State. Anyone who wants to satisfy their curiosity further will find the following representative publications and websites of special interest. You are cautioned not to stop with these, however. You will find thousands of additional resources in libraries, bookstores, and internet search engines.

Anyone interested in free information on travel and further details about California should contact the California Division of Tourism, 801 K Street, Suite 1600, Sacramento, CA 95814, 916-322-2881.

Print Publications

Brown, Ann Marie. *California Waterfalls.* San Francisco, CA: Foghorn Press, 1997.

Carter, Bob. *Food Festivals of Northern California.* Helena, MT: Falcon Publishing, 1997.

Carter, Bob. *Food Festivals of Southern California.* Helena, MT: Falcon Publishing, 1997.

Carter, Bob. *The Best of Central California.* Medina, WA: Johnson Associates International, 1995.

Clark, Jeanne. *California Wildlife Viewing Guide.* Helena, MT: Falcon Publishing, 1996.

Cooke, Anne Z. *Natural Wonders of Southern California: A Guide to Parks, Preserves & Wild Places.* Castine, ME: Country Roads Press, 1994.

Cunningham, Amy. *Grand Old Hotels of Northern California.* Kenmore, WA: Epicenter Press, Inc., 1996.

Gans, Liz, and Rick Newby. *Walking San Francisco.* Helena, MT: Falcon Publishing, 1999.

Gordon, William. *The Ultimate Hollywood Tour Book.* El Toro, CA: North Ridge Books, 1998.

Guddle, Erwin. *1000 California Place Names: Their Origin and Meaning.* Berkeley, CA: University of California Press, 1959.

Johnson, Marael. *California: Why Stop?: a Guide to California Roadside Historical Markers.* Houston, TX: Gulf Publishing Company, 1995.

Kelly, Leslie. *Traveling California's Gold Rush Country.* Helena, MT: Falcon Publishing, 1997.

Lee, Gregory. *The Best of Orange County.* Medina, WA: Johnson Associates International, 1993.

Martin, Don, and Betty Mastin. *California–Nevada Roads Less Traveled.* Henderson, NV: Pine Cone Press, 1999.

Moreno, Richard. *The Nevada Trivia Book.* Baldwin Park, CA: Gem Guides Book Company, 1998.

Nelson, Sharlene, and Ted Nelson. *Umbrella Guide to California Lighthouses.* Seattle, WA: Epicenter Press Inc., 1993.

Office of Historic Preservation. *California Historical Landmarks.* Sacramento, CA: California State Parks, 1996.

Ostertag, Rhonda, and George Ostertag. *California State Parks.* Seattle, WA: The Mountaineers, 1995.

Poshek, Lucy, and Roger Naylor. *California Trivia.* Nashville, TN: Rutledge Hill Press, 1998.

Roberts, Bruce, and Ray Jones. *California Lighthouses.* Guilford, CT: The Globe Pequot Press, 1997.

Strong, Kathy. *Southern California Off the Beaten Path.* Guilford, CT: The Globe Pequot Press, 1999.

Williams, Mark. *Northern California Off the Beaten Path.* Guilford, CT: The Globe Pequot Press, 1999.

Internet Websites:

http://donaldlaird.com/landmarks

http://ghosttowns.com

http://gocalif.ca.gov

www.byways.org

www.centralcoast-tourism.com

www.driveintheater.com

www.dumblaws.com

www.findagrave.com

www.homestead.com/travelbits

www.outwestnewspaper.com

www.seeing-stars.com

www.uselessknowledge.com